Alan

G000114354

Shadows on the Journey

the columba press

First published in 2011 by
the columba press
55A Spruce Avenue, Stillorgan Industrial Park,
Blackrock, Co Dublin

Cover by Bill Bolger
Origination by The Columba Press
Printed in Ireland by Gemini International, Dublin

ISBN 978 1 85607 736 1

Contents

Introduction

Throughout scripture there are many journeys recorded, by the children of Israel and by various individuals. There is also the journey of Jesus from Bethlehem to an empty tomb via the cross. In my own experience of faith and ministry, I have found myself on a journey with Jesus that has led me to places I never expected to be.

It has been important for me to reflect on that journey which has been exciting, demanding and at times exhausting. I have sought to follow a call that began a long time ago. I cannot separate my vocation and faith, as they are such a part of my struggle to live out my calling as a disciple. In these pages I seek to wrestle with the shadows that have been part of that pilgrimage. In reflecting upon the journey, I pray for strength and hope for what is still to come.

The theme throughout these reflections is that of shadows. Isaiah 25:5: 'as heat is reduced by the shadow of the cloud' and Isaiah 34:15: 'The owl will nest there and lay eggs, she will hatch them, and care for her young under the shadow of her wings.' The shadows on my journey have reminded me of one of my favourite words when I describe faith and try to make sense of it and that is 'paradox'. Some of the shadows that I have encountered have made my journey more difficult and indeed painful, as the light appears to have been hidden. However, even when I have not been aware of it, there has been a constant shadow with me, in the presence of Jesus. He has promised to be 'with us day after day after day'. (Matthew 28:20b)

Therefore my journey will reflect shadows that have brought darkness and difficulty, and shadows that have brought light and hope. My prayer is that as you read these thoughts you will find help as you live with the shadows that are part of your journey of faith, or even as you struggle with faith or live with no faith.

I am not sure where this journey of writing will lead me but it is in writing that I am able to discover those thoughts that are deep within me. As Henri Nouwen said: 'Writing is a process in which we discover what lives in us. The writing itself reveals what is alive ... The deepest satisfaction of writing is precisely that it opens up new spaces within us of which we were not aware before we started to write. To write is to embark on a journey whose final destination we do not know.' (From *Reflections on Theological Education*)

CHAPTER ONE

The Beginning and the End

I have often envied the first disciples – they saw, heard, touched and experienced the reality of Jesus. They were not left to read about him or have someone else to tell them what happened from their perspective. They were there and witnessed the evolving events as they happened and had an amazing mix of emotions: they were confused, upset, bewildered, bereaved and overjoyed. They experienced the roller coaster ride of following Jesus in first-century Palestine.

Their humanity is refreshing and helps me on my journey. They had their own perspective of what Jesus should do and be. He disappointed them, leaving them angry, hurting and hopeless. As some of them journeyed on the road to Emmaus they began to see things differently. The shadows lifted as they were accompanied by the one who had shadowed them on their journey. It was only when they began to understand that 'the story was never about Israel beating up her enemies and becoming established as the high-and-mighty masters of the world. It was always the story of how the creator God, Israel's covenant God, would bring the saving purposes for the world to birth through the suffering and vindication of Israel.' (N. T. Wright in *The Challenge of Jesus*, pp 123-4) Jesus had to help them see the horror of Good Friday from a different perspective. They had made understandable assumptions and could not grasp what had happened. Patiently, from the scriptures they knew and loved, he showed them a very different backcloth that made sense of what had taken place and enabled them to see differently and discover that resurrection had happened.

This is the beginning for me of recognising that the story that enabled me to believe and have faith to follow Jesus was at first someone else's story, and in time I have had to become part of the story. I have also had to filter some of the assumptions I was given and find the amazing grace and mercy of God in Jesus, who has been the constant shadow even when I have not realised it.

There has never been a time in my journey that I did not believe in God, but there have been times when I was keen not to recognise the challenge of seeking to live it. I can remember those critical influences that helped me find my connection with the journey of faith. There was the influence of family that caused me to see that there was a trust in God even in the most difficult of circumstances. Somehow or other God was still present in human pain and was not blamed for it but became a source of strength to enable my mum to cope. This faith was not trumpeted or forced; in fact it was almost hidden because of a sense of unworthiness. As I understand it now, this unease was caused by other people's faith perspective that was so forcefully projected that it was assumed to be true. As someone who was separated from her husband, the perception was that she was a real sinner compared to others who were self righteous. John Shore in his book *Penguins, Pain and the whole Shebang,* NY 2005, p 69) writes:

> Why are so many Christians so obnoxious and mean spirited? It seems like Christianity is mostly about being judgemental, narrow-minded, and having an infuriatingly condescending attitude toward anyone who isn't a Christian. Christians are so busy being Christian that they forget to be kind.

The Jesus presented to me in my childhood, through various religious and church activities, was someone who was interested in helping me to know that I needed to be rescued from my sin. And he would give me a perfect life in heaven after this life. The emphasis in this life appeared to be about telling others how to escape eternal punishment in the world to come. This shadow often left me with a huge burden of guilt, of never being good enough, of not recognising the amazing love that God had for me. The wonder of grace was lost in the awfulness of my humanity. Steve Chalke describes this in the following way:

> Countless people have received the impression that God

doesn't like humanity very much and that he is utterly disillusioned with us. I've given up trying to keep track of the number of people I have spoken to, young and old, who tell me through tears, 'I'm too sinful for God to ever be interested in me'. The double tragedy is that many of these are Christians who have been in our churches for years. Millions of people, both inside and outside the church, are paralysed by the thought that God is angry with them and might smite them at any moment.' (*Intelligent Church*, p 53)

I find myself smiling when I read Richard Rohr writing: 'The great and merciful surprise is that we come to God not by doing it right but by doing it wrong'. (*Everything Belongs*, p 21) Julian of Norwich states: 'Sin shall not be a shame to humans, but a glory … The mark of sin shall be turned to honour.' (chapter 38, Showing 13 of *Revelations of Divine Love*) The paradoxes of faith excite me – the kingdom of God turns so many of our perceptions upside down and inside out. It is my brokenness and inability to live as I want to that helps me discover the amazing mercy of God. I can rejoice at how I mess up because it helps me to experience the joy of being forgiven.

I have had to leave behind the shadow of certainty for the shadow of mystery. Richard Rohr writes: 'Religion has not tended to create seekers or searchers, has not tended to create honest humble people who trust that God is always beyond them. We aren't focused on the great mystery. Rather religion has tended to create people who think they have God in their pockets, people with quick easy, glib answers. If the great mystery is the Great Mystery, it will lead us into paradox, into darkness, and into journeys that never cease.' (pp 35-36) This discovery of the wonder of God and how we can never fully understand or explain our faith, has helped me find excitement in the struggle. To be cherished by a God who is way beyond my comprehension has been liberating. Eugene Peterson writes: 'God cannot be defined. "Yahweh" is not a definition. God cannot be reduced to an "object" of our inquiry or search. Is the name purposely enigmatic? Reflectional but not telling everything? Disclosing intimacy, personal presence, but preserving mystery, forbidding possession and control?' (*Christ Plays in Ten Thousand Places*, p 159)

This faith that allows mystery and questions has given me energy and vitality on my journey, but it has also meant that I may be misunderstood. Questions and struggle can be viewed by some fellow travellers as weakness or as a lack of faith. Jesus, in journeying with the disciples to Emmaus, was patient with their confusion, he gave them space and time to talk and to question. He wanted them to have faith, not certainty. He encouraged them to explore and discover. He modelled faith as sometimes difficult and even at times bewildering. I have never been so confident of the love and presence of Jesus with me on my journey, but I don't have the answers I used to have, and the questions are not as important. The shadow of mystery keeps me probing and questioning as I wrestle with scripture, read about other people's understanding and reflect upon my own experience of seeking to live out faith that is based on relationship with the one who journeys with us. Richard Rohr writes: 'Religious energy is in the dark questions, seldom in the answers. Answers are the way out, but that is not what we are here for. But when we look at the questions, we look for the opening to transformation.' (*Everything Belongs*, p 45)

In my development in faith I was particularly concerned about disconnection between faith and the complex issues of hatred, violence and political polarisation. As I witnessed riots, people being burnt out of their homes, bombs, bullets and murders, this was being described as a religious war. Atrocities were presented as being against by Protestants against Catholics or by Catholics against Protestants. My experience of growing up through 'The Troubles' left me questioning the connection between the gospel and local culture. My culture, as a Protestant growing up in East Belfast, emphasised the need for personal salvation and the life hereafter, and yet the injustice and violence did not appear to have any connection with the gospel, or if it did it could be to ensure the other side was put down. Increasingly I came to question how the good news must impinge upon our attitudes to all people, even to those who were seen as the enemy, or just plain different. This growing belief was affirmed by people I formed friendships with who came from different religious and cultural backgrounds. So often the churches appeared to be part of the divide, rather than prophetically questioning it.

As Brian McLaren writes in *The Secret Message of Jesus* (p 84): 'We may have talked about going to heaven after we die, but not about God's will being done on earth before we die. We may have pressurised people to be moral and good or correct and orthodox to avoid hell after death, but we didn't inspire them with the possibility of becoming beautiful and fruitful to heal the earth in this life.' Over the years I have found the truth of scripture when St Paul wrote: 'You are all children of God through faith in Christ Jesus, for all of you who were baptised into Christ have clothed yourselves with Christ. There is neither Jew nor Greek, slave nor free, male nor female, for you are all one in Christ Jesus.' (Galatians 3:26-28)

The darkness of this shadow was heightened by the fact that the spiritual heritage I was given taught me that my journey was about God and me; there was no clear understanding of the body of Christ, that we cannot do this or should do this on our own. The concept of 'Our Father' was lost in individual piety. The faith heritage I received had for sometime failed to ac- knowledge the gift of *koinonia*, 'the body of Christ', how we have so much to give to one another and that together we are so much stronger – we are not meant to journey alone. Marion Leach Jacobsen writes in her book, *Crowded Pews and Lonely People*, (Tyndale House, 1975): 'Our churches are filled with people who outwardly look contented and at peace but inwardly are crying out for someone to love them … just as they are – con- fused, frustrated, often frightened, guilty, and often unable to communicate even within their own families. But the other peo- ple in the church look so happy and contented that one seldom has the courage to admit his own deep needs before such a self- sufficient group as the average church meeting appears to be.'

I am very grateful, as I have journeyed, for the companions who have given me permission to ask questions and given me the space to grow and change. These have been friends who have been able to affirm me and give me space to struggle and probe, not just to accept other people's perception of what this journey is, but to help me be part of the story and yet allow me to be true to myself. They have been shadows that have protected me and enabled me to rest from the heat, and help me know the presence of Jesus by being him to me. They have and still do form the shield of faith for me and that is what we are called to do as together we pray, 'Our Father'. We belong to each other and need to recognise how important the gifts of affirmation and encouragement are on the journey. There is something very beautiful about friendships that are rooted in Jesus as they give light and hope, they allow us to experience the accepting love and mercy of him who calls us to follow on this difficult journey where there is no map and only general instructions.

I have been intrigued with the various people I have encountered who have shared their lives and faith stories with me. There has been such a rich variety of people who have experienced the presence of God with them in some very difficult places. Over the last thirty years, I have been privileged to share with many often in the most painful and sad chapters of their lives. I have wept with them and encouraged them to express their anger and disappointment with God, and yet through those dark moments I have been humbled by how they have found some light in their darkness and some peace in their torment. I do not have any answers to the suffering and the randomness of what happens, but I have been given glimpses into the mystery that God is present in so much of what appears to be hell itself. The scriptures also reflect this concern that God has for the widow, the orphan, the hungry, the poor and those in prison. One of the most uncomfortable parables for me is that found in St Matthew's gospel, the parable of the sheep and the goats. I always find myself disturbed by this parable and wonder how many times I have failed to be Jesus to those in need.

It is this critical connection between what we say and what we do, in fact who we are, that I have found to be a shadow on my journey. I am concerned that in our religious culture the Christian community has often lost sight of what I call the incarnational good news. We are meant to be the real presence of Jesus in our local communities, to make a difference. I believe we need to find a holy discontentment, Jürgen Moltmann writes about hope in the following way: 'Those who hope in Christ can no longer put up with reality as it is, but begin to suffer under it, to contradict it. Peace with God means conflict in the world, for the goal of the promised future stabs inexorably into the flesh of every unfulfilled present.' (*Theology of Hope*, p 21)

This struggle for me has become all the more important because for most of my adult life I have journeyed with Jesus as
someone who is in ordained ministry. So much time in parish
ministry is taken up looking after people who belong to the
church, rather than helping the church, 'God's people', to make
connections at every level with the local community in which
we were called to live and thereby serve. Bishop Penny
Jamieson describes this connection: 'We badly need to rediscover
the conection between our churches and the communities in
which they stand, to re-find the gift of 'gossiping the gospel', to
know what we are committed to and stand firm without com-
promise, but without judgement of those who cannot join us.
We need constantly to turn with loving eyes onto God's world,
ready to engage at depth with the longing for significance and
meaning in life that is the lot of all humankind.' (*Living at the
Edge*, p 153)

I will return to this and some other shadows I have mentioned in this first chapter. However I want to acknowledge that
my struggle has been enriched and made much more difficult
because I am ordained, and even more so since I was ordained
as a bishop. My own journey is so wrapped up in the ministry to
which I believe I am called to. This has wonderful opportunites
but also huge responibilities. This has been a shadow in itself
and indeed this book is being written at a time when I am recovering from the demands of that ministry. There are lessons in
that for me that are profound, but there are also insights which I
have, and which I want to share with others. I have found the
following words very helpful: 'We do not really know God except through our broken and rejoicing humanity.' (*Everything
Belongs*, Richard Rohr, p 19) This is one of the shadows that I
find intriguing. I, like many others, have found Jesus more present with me when I am struggling, and I believe that is because
it helps me recognise how dependent I am upon his grace and
peace.

CHAPTER TWO

To Belong or not Belong

Remembering is a fascinating exercise, particularly when done in a group, when everybody has a slightly different take on the events. When I was a young teenager I played for our parish church football team and we managed to get to a junior cup final. In my memory I remember that final with some embarrassment, as I scored the most wonderful own goal. It was meant to be a pass back to our goalkeeper! The goalkeeper was very quick to remember that the goal he conceded was not his fault. Our goal scorers remember how brilliant their contribution was. Other members of that team remember the joy of winning the cup, as we eventually won the game 2-1.

During my days in youth groups attached to my parish church, scripture was taken very seriously. I was delighted to carry a Bible and to show how much it meant to me. For those who taught me I am forever grateful that they taught me the importance of this tool for the journey. However, there was difficulty in asking questions about what was said. It was assumed that creation did take place in seven days and that evolution was just a scientific theory. There was no attempt at serious debate. It appeared that every word written was literally true, and it was in the King James Version. As I wrestled with this, I felt that scripture was a shadow that I needed to make sense of for myself. There were issues I wanted to question and find a way of making sense of this 'word of God', that did justice to the revelation that I was thrilled to read. I did not and could not accept other people's interpretations. I needed to respect other views but also be true to my own understanding. In a religious culture this is difficult because people seem to feel threatened when you ask difficult questions. Some people almost appeared to take it personally. It was easier to dismiss me than to deal with the genuine searching.

This is a continuing struggle on my journey. I love the scriptures, they form part of my daily devotions, I preach from them, they excite me, they disturb me, they confuse and they thrill me. The critical thing for me is to see them in context as part of God's revelation to us. They are not of themselves the 'word of God', but become to us life-giving and transforming as the Holy Spirit brings them to life. In his book, *Threshold of the Future*, Michael Riddell writes: 'The Bible is not the word of God. It may contain the word of God, in a way that a womb contains a baby. But the womb is not the baby. Scripture may become the word of God under the inspiration of the Spirit, and often does. But it is heretical and idolatrous to imagine that the word of the living God can be objectified in such a way that it exists within and is limited by a set of printed words on a page. The word of God is the self-communication of God, and therefore is dynamically connected to the person of God. One cannot know the word of God without knowing God.' I have had to study the scriptures as an academic exercise as part of ordination training, and also by personal choice, but knowing about the scriptures is very different from knowing the word of life who is revealed through the hidden depths of the record we have been given in the Bible. That is a search that demands questioning and openness to the Holy Spirit who brings the pages to life for us.

As someone who finds silence and contemplation a rich part of my own spiritual journey, I have found the ancient Christian tradition of *lectio divina* a helpful way of reading scripture. '*Lectio divina* is an 'active' kind of reading in this sense: we are not just passive listeners to what God has said and done in the past. The words are addressed to us, and we are expected to do something. They are one side of a conversation, to which our prayer and lives are the response. *Lectio divina* is a way of praying, but a prayer where we let God start a conversation, rather than when we are constantly bombarding God with our own agenda and preoccupations.' (*Reading with God*, David Foster OSB, p 1) It is in the silence and the listening that we might just discern the word of God for us on our journey.

It is not just views on the Bible that cause division and disagreement within 'the body of Christ'. Having grown up in a deeply divided society that had a religious backcloth, I was always aware of the problem of religious conflict. However, it was only as I moved into adult life that I became conscious of the many and varied difficulties between God's people, and not just between Catholic and Protestant. This has been a dark shadow on my journey, as I believe profoundly in the scripture that we are all one in Christ (Galatians 3:28) and that Jesus himself commands our oneness and unity (John 17:21).

The World Christian Database numbers over 9,000 denominations, while the World Christian Encyclopaedia comes up with 33,820! It appears to be the case that, over many years, when Christians disagree with one another they simply form another denomination or sect. What is it about those of us who believe, that we can argue or indeed fight with each other with such ease? It really does the message we say we believe in so much damage. Our integrity and that of the Jesus we say we love is questioned and I find this shadow a very dark one on my journey. There are some who would doubt the reality of my faith because of my willingness to pray and worship with others. The irony for me is that I have often found more of Jesus and his grace in those I am meant not to accept than in those who question my actions.

One of my earliest examples of this was when I was a student at Queen's University in Belfast. At that stage of my own faith journey, I was beginning to discern a call to ordination and because of my upbringing and local parish I assumed that it would be in the Church of Ireland. I was part of a small department fellowship group where we studied and prayed together. It was part of the university Christian Union. When I mentioned that I had begun a process of discernment with the Church of Ireland that might lead to ordination, two members of the group who were concerned for my wellbeing, took me out for coffee and a scone. They were not sure how God could be calling me into ministry in that particular church, as in Northern Ireland terms 'there was a paper thin wall between us and the Roman Catholic Church'. In other words, their perception was that I was mishearing God because God couldn't be wrong. I could spend time discussing much of their sentiments and belief, but suffice to say, I didn't take their advice but thanked them for their concern and asked them to pray for me.

From my perspective, in some Christian thinking there is too much time spent on assessing others and their faith. Richard Rohr writes: 'Group-think is a substitute for God-think. We believe that God is only found by our group. We then claim that identification with our group is the only way to serve God. When the way becomes an end in itself, it becomes idolatry. In idolatry the religious concern is 'Who is on my way?' and 'Who is saying it my way?' The ones who say it my way are good, the others are bad.' (*Everything Belongs*, pp 94-5) Too often denominations and groups develop a group identity or mentality that becomes more important than the essence of any faith journey, and that is relationship with God in Jesus. The dynamic of relationship is about growth, change, struggle and learning new insights. I would even go as far to say that sometimes it will mean changing my mind and even admitting I was wrong.

It is not just between various denominations and Christian groups that there are divisions but also within them. As an Anglican I am deeply aware of the pain and hurt within our Communion. I was a very new bishop when I was privileged to attend the Lambeth Conference held in Canterbury in 2008. It was an incredible experience to realise how we are part of such a worldwide body of fellow disciples. There was deep pain expressed at that gathering and a sadness at so many bishops not attending because of personal conscience. This is not the place to discuss the complex issues of the Anglican Communion but I do mention one of the insights from that experience that was important for me. It is the tension between culture and gospel. What is in essence of the gospel? What is cultural, particularly in a local setting? How do we ensure that culture doesn't replace gospel? Yet how do we ensure the gospel doesn't lose credibility in a local culture? These are complex and difficult questions but I witnessed so many arguments where these questions where at the heart of the debate and there was no easy answer.

My memory of my mum's struggle with this was expressed in her concern that as a teenager her generation shouldn't dance or wear make-up, not to mention going to a pub. This was surely a cultural taboo rather than an essential part of discipleship. In my generation it was about whether a Christian could drink alcohol or about not wearing jeans to go to church. These are again cultural issues that can cause so much hot air and unnecessary hurt, rejection and judgement.

Some of these cultural questions have been made more pronounced by visits I have made to Kenya and Uganda. How much of what missionaries taught was gospel and how much was a process of Westernisation? Why do African Anglicans wear robes that were for weather in the UK? Why do they chant canticles that stop their natural and wonderful rhythm? I have experienced processing up an aisle in Kenya to African dance music and that was a wonderful expression of African culture. Leslie Newbigin describes this struggle: 'The Jesus whom he thus accepts will be the Jesus presented to him by the missionary. It will be Jesus as the missionary perceives him. The convert, having realised that much of what he had first accepted from the missionary was shaped by the latter's culture and not solely by the gospel, may in reaction turn back to his own culture and seek, in a sort of hostile reaction to the culture that had invaded his own under the cloak of the gospel, to restate the gospel in terms of his own traditional culture.' (*Foolishness to the Greeks*, pp 8 and 9) This shadow leads me to constantly question in our own culture what is of gospel and what is of culture. This is particularly important because increasingly I believe the churches have disconnected from local communities and many non-church-goers see us as irrelevant, out of date and that we should be consigned to the past. I will return to some of these issues in a later chapter.

As a student I had the delight of visiting different churches, partly because of various friends but mainly out of curiosity. There is such a diverse way of 'doing church' and yet within each place of worship there was a liturgy. There would be denominations who believe they do not have a liturgy, but their structure and style is the same every week. They have a form that they follow and, even though songs, hymns, prayers and readings may vary, there is a similar pattern each week. Within the different denominations there was also a variety of theological outlooks. Within my frame of reference I experienced evangelical, catholic, charismatic, conservative and liberal. A rich variety of Christian expressions still exists today but my concern then and now is that there is often an unhealthy competition and division between them, weakening the witness of Christ's command for unity.

I find myself wanting to embrace various strengths from differing strands of the Christian church, and yearn for God's people to find something of Jesus in each other, no matter what label we may give others. Brian McLaren writes: 'For too many people the name Jesus has become a symbol of exclusion, as if Jesus' statement 'I am the way, and the truth, and the life; no one comes to the Father except through me' actually means, 'I am in the way of people seeking truth and life. I won't let anyone get to God unless he comes through me.' The name of Jesus, whose life resonated with acceptance, welcome and inclusion, has too often become a symbol of elitism, exclusion and aggression.' (*A Generous Orthodoxy*, p 70)

My home parish, Willowfield Parish in East Belfast, gave me a solid grounding in faith from an evangelical perspective. I learnt a love of scripture and the need for a personal response to the amazing love of God made known in Jesus. From my charismatic friends and experiences, I learnt a freedom in the Spirit in prayer and in praying for others, where the gifts of the Spirit can be used wisely and carefully. In my ecumenical journey I have learnt from the richness of the catholic tradition, the need for spiritual direction, the awe and wonder of the sacrament and the real presence of Jesus. There is no doubt in my experience that Jesus is present in the Eucharist; the problem comes when we try to define the mystery. From my conservative friends I am reminded of the daily difficulty I and all of humanity have with sin. From a liberal perspective I am reminded that there are issues where there is not a black and white answer (I like grey!). There is also a reminder of the social element of the gospel: the gospel is about incarnation and must be relational, not just correct words or belief, as faith in Jesus is at its heart relationship. 'For the language of faith is not primarily interested in communicating information (Jesus did not come as a scientist or theologian), but in forming healthy, healing, transformative relationships.' (Peter Rollins, *The Orthodox Heretic*, p 42)

These various denominations, groups and theological outlooks have been a shadow on the journey of faith for me, sometimes providing light and sometimes darkness. There has been light when I have been able to learn from others and find something of the richness we have to give each other to help us on our respective journeys. However, the darkness has been when certain outlooks have become exclusive and judgemental. 'There can be no mission where there is no contact, and many Christians in the West today are imprisoned and isolated by an unnecessary concern for their own sanctification. These bearers of the precious "treasure" of Christ's presence have become locked into a theological outlook which prevents them from sharing it with the people who are most hungry and "sick".' (Michael Riddell, *Threshold of the Future*, p 85)

I have found that the gift of friendship and soul sharing to be wonderful gifts as I journey. I am very glad that we are not called to live out this faith on our own, but God has given so many companions for the journey, people who are at different places on the journey and some who do not believe the validity of the journey. 'Salvation is not a private deal with God. We are bound by the action of God in Christ to the entire creation that 'waits with eager longing for the revealing of the children of God.' (Rom 8:19) Any understanding of salvation that separates us from others is false and sooner or later cripples our participation in what God in Christ is doing in history, saving the world.' (Eugene Peterson, *Christ Plays in Ten Thousand Places*, p 211)

Increasingly I believe that those of us who are on this journey of faith with Jesus have to rediscover something of the joy and excitement in following him, but also the incredible challenge in ensuring we are expressing the radical and life-changing message that Jesus would bring to today's world. John Pritchard describes this in the following way:

> Many social factors are running in the opposite direction to the church's health, and at the same time we in the church seem to have decided various ecclesiastical games instead of trusting Jesus and giving our attention to the world. One writer illustrates the danger like this. Say you invite Jesus to share your home. It's huge fun and leads to lots of laughter as well as stimulating conversation and changes in the running of the house. However, after a while you find Jesus poring over adverts for Christian Aid and Oxfam in the daily

paper, and then looking around your well-appointed home, and you begin to feel just a bit uncomfortable. You want to take him to church, of course, and that goes well. They love his fresh energy and openness. However, they do find some of what he does worryingly relaxed – even casual. He wants to ask questions in the sermon; he doesn't seem very bothered about some of the conventions and rituals we value; he sings too loudly, almost as if he means it. So the churchwardens wonder if he'd like to try another church down the road. At home he continues to be great company, but he does bring some strange friends back to the house. Finally it all comes to a head when he brings back an entire family of asylum seekers and gives them his room while he sleeps on the landing. It's no good. You decide you'll have to put him in a cupboard, for safety. So that's what you do, and you put a cross and two candles outside the cupboard so people will know he's in there – but not dangerous.' (*Living Jesus*, p 78)

CHAPTER THREE

Shadows Within

With hindsight, I can reflect on the understanding of faith that I was given as a child and teenager. The joy of discovering new things is exhilarating but with the delight comes the struggle of questioning and the hard work of thinking and praying for yourself. Too often faith is something that we have received, but we fail to wrestle with it and thereby put down deep roots, so that in the crisis we will stand firm.

One of the issues that I struggled with on my journey is the paradox of knowing I am 'made in the image of God' and yet I 'have fallen short of the glory of God'. Near our home in East Belfast was a place called 'Daddy Winker's Lane', and it was a shortcut home for me from primary school. Along this lane there was a playground with swings, a witch's hat and a see-saw. My favourite was the see-saw. It was huge and there was enough room for seven or eight children to sit on either end. The task was to get the see-saw to carry the other end as high as possible. There were those occasions when the two sides were so well balanced that we could keep the see-saw in the middle with all of us having our feet off the ground. This must have been my genetic history as an Anglican, as I enjoyed the middle ground where there was balance.

My background meant I was very aware of original sin and how bad I was, and if I believed, I would escape the eternal punishment that was rightly mine. The problem with much that passes for religious teaching is that there may be elements of truth, but unfortunately we may only hear part of the truth. Grace is paramount on our faith journey. I do not believe that Jesus died because I and all of humanity are so bad, but because of the amazing grace and love God has for the whole created order, expressed beautifully and poignantly by the life, death and resurrection of Jesus.

Eugene Peterson writes:

'A primary but often shirked task of the Christian in our society and culture is to notice, to see in detail, the sacredness of creation. The marks of God's creative work are all around us and in us. We live surrounded by cherubim singing Holy, Holy, Holy. It is easy to miss it. Sin-graffiti disfigure both land and people. Death is a frequent visitor. Blasphemies assault our ears. And our sin-blurred eyes and sin-dulled ears miss the glory that is right before us. But no excuses. We have a huge responsibility and an enormous privilege to live daily in such a way that we give witness to the immense and sacred gifts of time and place.' (*Christ Plays in Ten Thousand Places*, p 85)

This captures part of the truth that I never received when I was younger. I am someone who fails to do the things I want to and I do the things I don't want to do, but I am nonetheless made in the image of God and in Jesus am a child of God. I want to shout 'Wow!' Part of my struggle on my journey is to break free from the shadow of my brokenness and learn to dance in the wonderful shadow of God's amazing grace.

This is a discovery that I need to keep returning to, because I am still haunted by the need to feel guilty. So much of my early journey was about being guilty and not being good enough. The miracle of our faith, the joy and delight of what we have been given is that we fail, but forgiveness is a gift freely given. I have met so many people throughout my years in ordained ministry who have believed all their lives that they are not good enough, and will not even receive holy communion because they will never be good enough. Part of the travesty of it is that, this is how they have been made to feel by those who claim to be Christian. My mum told me, on more than one occasion, she didn't go to church to hear how bad she was, but to get some hope that she could be better!

William Stringfellow, an American lawyer who has written some wonderful theological reflections, pens the following:

'The worth of a man's life is bestowed as the gift of God's wholly gratuitous love for man, decisively manifested in

history in Christ. In this sense, without getting into the contro-
versies of the Reformation, all Christians can speak of justification by faith rather than by works. This justification is unconditional; it is not modified by the aspirations or achievements
of men. It is not the prize for any accomplishments and not the
consequence of any sacrifices. Undeserved, unearned, immeas-
urable, free and priceless.' (*Impostors of God*, pp 6 and 7)

All of us have a different genetic profile and have a different
life history. My genes mean that I am not very tall and have had
a receding hair line for a few years now. My personal history
means that I have acquired certain attitudes and thought
processes and even certain patterns of behaviour. I cannot leave
the house without checking I have locked the door at least once,
for which I am forever grateful to my mum as I still imagine her
whispering in my ear, 'did you lock the door?' The circumstances of my family during my childhood has obviously had an
impact on my thinking and actions. My dad essentially disap-
peared when I was six, and one of the dark shadows on my pilgrimage has been a difficulty with the concept of 'Our Father'.
Trusting God has been a constant challenge for me. I imagine
that he will let me down or just not be there. This has been a constant theme of my personal prayer journey, learning slowly and
painfully that I can trust in the grace and mercy of God. I have
found the writings of Henri Nouwen have inspired me, especially his reflections on Rembrandt's painting.

'Instead of its being called 'The Return of the Prodigal Son', it
could have easily been called 'The Welcome by the
Compassionate Father.' The emphasis is less on the son than
on the father. The parable is in truth a 'Parable of the Father's
Love'. Looking at the way in which Rembrandt portrays the
father, there came to me a whole new interior understanding
of tenderness, mercy, and forgiveness. Seldom, if ever, has
God's immense, compassionate love been expressed in such
a poignant way. I also see, however, infinite compassion, unconditional love, everlasting forgiveness – divine realities –
emanating from a Father who is the creator of the universe.'
(*The Return of the Prodigal Son*, p 92)

This profound understanding of God's unconditional love is something like a dripping tap that has slowly but surely made its way into my consciousness, and enabled me to believe that God is with me always. It is important to note that my mum's great lesson that even in the most painful places God is present, must be added at this point. God's love does not mean that we will find life a perfectly scripted story. There are no guarantees on this journey except God's love and the promise to be with us. This wonderful realisation of the enormity and joy of God's love for me as his child has been a shadow that has protected and sheltered me on the journey.

John Main describes the wonder of this journey in the following way:

> All of us are sinners. All of us are capable of sin and of the desire for sin. All of us have sinned and do sin. But what is of supreme importance for every one of us is that we come into the presence of Jesus, we are strengthened by him, and our egotism is deflated by the sheer beauty of his being. This journey is a journey away from self, away from egotism, away from selfishness, away from isolation. It is a journey into the infinite love of God. With some of us, the end of egotism requires a big struggle. Sometimes, we are carried more or less kicking and screaming into the kingdom of heaven.' (quoted in *John Main: The Expanding Vision*, ed L. Freeman and S. Reynolds, pp 33-34)

I am not sure if it is learned behaviour or was just in my genes, but from a young age I am very aware of other people's pain. I have been given a gift of intuition and indeed compassion for fellow strugglers. This has been a wonderful help in pastoral ministry, enabling me to journey with people who are in that most difficult place of human suffering. It is the randomness of suffering that is so difficult to make sense of. There are those who do appear to have more than their fair share. I have never found any answers to the 'why question', but paradoxically I have found the reality of God's presence in what appears to be hell itself. The mystery of suffering is something that has been a shadow on my journey, mainly because when I was at the beginning of my journey of faith, I was taught and believed that everything must be God's will. I have seen too much of the randomness of pain, and I profoundly disagree with this now, as it paints a very harsh and cruel God who appears to pick on people indiscriminately, and it doesn't do justice to the unanswered questions in scripture.

For some reason, since my childhood I have always wanted to help people in pain, to support and care. I am sure it came from watching my mum struggle to cope with what happened to her. However, somewhere along the way I also adopted the idea that I have to fix it for others. As I reflect upon this now, I am also conscious that there has been at times a Messiah complex – it is up to me to sort it. This has been a difficult admission but has come at a time when I am recovering from years of giving and seeking to be compassionate. In returning to the gospels I find it staggering that Jesus, when he came and dwelt among us, didn't fix life for everyone. He healed many but there were also many he didn't. His special gift was the gift of his presence among us. Being here is the essence of the birth of a baby in a manger, in a stable in Bethlehem. Throughout his ministry there is that wonderful balance between doing and being. He was with people so much that he had to withdraw to a lonely place to pray and to recover. This is a struggle for me, I want to help and care for people but I need to learn to say 'no' and to ensure I take time to withdraw and recover. Availability is good but without some space it can be dangerous for those who are offering themselves in service to others. Phil Simmons, a young man, terminally ill, wrote the following:

> 'As I see it we are truly grown up when we stop trying to fix people … Before we go fixing others, we must first accept and find compassion for ourselves. Doing so we may begin to find that others don't need "fixing" so much as simple kindness. When we stop seeing the world as a "Problem" to be solved, when instead we open our hearts to the mystery of our common suffering, we may find ourselves where we least expected to be: in a world transformed by love.' (*Learning to Fall: The Blessings of an Imperfect Life*, Bantam Books, 2002)

The shadow of my childhood still haunts me. I want to fix people's pain but there is the danger that that is more about my need to be needed and loved than it is about bringing Jesus to others. I cannot fix people's suffering but I can by my presence bring the grace and love of God to them, just by being there.

As an introvert and someone who enjoys contemplation and silence, those moments of withdrawal are critical because they force me to recognise my own brokenness and need for healing and help. In the monastic tradition, this place of reflection is known as the cell or cave. There is at present a rediscovery of many of the values and benefits of the monastic life. I have found great benefit in visiting the Benedictine Monastery in Rostrevor, for the rhythm of worship, silence and hospitality. This holy place has helped me and many others find the space for restoration and renewal. I am very grateful to the brothers for their welcome and prayers. To be able to leave the busyness and frenetic activity of doing, just to be, is a special gift and a necessary resource for spiritual well being. Ian Adams paints a picture of the monastic tradition beautifully: 'This is life rooted in stillness, prayer and simplicity, practised by people of the desert, of the cell, of the cave. This is the place of self-revelation and the site of God-encounter.' The ancient Jewish writer puts it rather more starkly:

> to sit alone in silence
> When the Lord has imposed it,
> To put one's mouth to the dust-
> There may yet be hope.
> (Lamentations 3:28-29 NRSV)

The busyness of church life has often been a concern for me. It is usually the same people who show any interest that are railroaded into doing more than they should and often they become weary in well-doing. I believe we need to make more time for listening, for being, for allowing God to do what God does, and enable ourselves to not get in the way. There is the danger that we think God cannot do things without us rather than the truth, which is, we can do nothing without him.

I want to leave the shadow of busyness and restless activity and find the shadow of stillness and being, so that God can be God. That is something that is not easy to do, especially in public ministry where the expectations and demands of others are constantly screaming your attention. Karl Barth is said to have writ-

ten: 'A being is free only when it can determine and limit its activity.' There are times when I have found myself doing many
things and just about juggling them all, but I find it much harder
to do nothing. There is something of the shadow of guilt haunting
me at that point. It is fascinating to discover how many of these
shadows overlap and impinge upon each other. That is why the
place of stillness and silence is so important, to give space for
being that I would find it difficult to do because of being busy.

My experience has taught me yet another paradox on this
faith journey. Henri Nouwen writes: 'The great paradox of love
is that precisely when you have claimed yourself as God's
beloved child, have set boundaries to your love, and thus contained your needs, you begin to grow into the freedom to give
gratuitously' (*The Inner Voice of Love*, p 10) My security, my
stronghold is the knowledge that I am cherished by God. The
children's hymn puts it so simply and profoundly:

Jesus loves me this I know,
For the bible tells me so.

In knowing and grasping something of this amazing love I
want to pray as follows:

Dear Jesus,
Help us to spread your fragrance everywhere we go.
Flood our souls with your spirit and life.
Penetrate and possess our whole being so utterly that our
lives may only be a radiance of yours.
Shine through us, and so be in us, that every soul we come
into contact with may feel your presence in our soul.
Let them look up and see no longer us but only Jesus!
Stay with us, and then we shall begin to shine as you shine;
so to shine as to be a light to others; the light of O Jesus, will
be all from you, none of it will be ours; it will be you shining
on others through us.
Let us praise you in the way you love best by shining on
those around us.
Let us preach you without preaching, not by words but by
our example, by the catching force, the sympathetic influence of what we do.

The evident fullness of the love our hearts bear to you.
Amen.'
(quoted in *Becoming the answer to our Prayers* by S. Claiborne
and J. Wilson-Hartgrove, p 114)

32

CHAPTER FOUR

Yes ... But!

I have often been asked why? The answer is different depending
on the context and on the person asking the question. However,
there is a thread that runs through any answer and that is reluctance. I have lived with this question for so long that it is a massive part of my journey. Why was I ordained?

It is difficult to remember when it began, as I was struggling
with being on any journey with Jesus for much of my teenage
years. It was initially the more important question. With a growing clarity in my recognition of a call to be a disciple despite my
reluctant response, then came the questioning how this discipleship would be lived out. This is a constant theme on my journey,
that my first calling is to be a disciple and from that a call to
ordination grew. In the religious context that I grew up in, this
can often be misunderstood. Frederick Buechner writes: 'If you
tell me Christian commitment is a kind of thing that has happened to you once and for all, like some kind of spiritual plastic
surgery, I say go to, go to, you're either pulling the wool over
your own eyes or trying to pull it over mine. Every morning you
should wake up in your bed and ask yourself: "Can I believe it
all again today?" No, better still, don't ask it till after you've
read *The New York Times*, till after you've studied that daily
record of the world's brokenness and corruption, which should
always stand beside your Bible. Then ask yourself if you can believe in the gospel of Jesus Christ again for that particular day.'
(*From the Return of Ansel Gibbs*)

I have struggled at times to deal with the certainty of what
people can describe as faith, where there are only answers to
questions people aren't asking, where there are pious and in-
sulting answers to people's pain. There are so many times I cannot make sense of what is happening and I don't have any answers, but somehow, in the midst of the mess, Jesus is present.

That is where my faith gives me strength and hope, but not answers and certainty.

I have never been more convinced of the reality of Jesus but I am concerned as to how we so often present the faith to others. Jesus in the gospels exhibits an amazing gift of enabling people to relate to him and sense something of who he is, and it is from this relational experience that faith might just blossom. Jesus being present was much more important than answering questions or preaching at people. He gained the opportunity to speak by being with people in their context and without judgement. The incarnation is critical for us in our present culture where people have become cynical about the church and thereby about Jesus. In my youth the Christian influence I received was very concerned with spiritual needs, to the neglect of societal and justice issues, not least in the dreadful sectarianism tearing at the soul of our communities. This was the context in which I was wrestling with my call to be a disciple. Brian McLaren pens the following commentary which applies to my experience: 'More and more reflective Christian leaders are beginning to realise that, for the millions of young adults who dropped out of their churches in the late twentieth and early twenty-first centuries, the Christian religion appears to be a failed religion. It has specialised in people's destination in the afterlife but has failed to address significant social injustices in this life. It has focused on 'me' and 'my soul' and 'my spiritual life' and 'my eternal destiny', but is has failed to address the dominant societal and global issues of their lifetime: systemic injustice, systemic poverty, systemic ecological crisis, systemic dysfunction of many kinds.' (*Everything Must Change*, p 33)

This was a shadow from which I emerged convinced that I was to be a disciple of Jesus. There is such joy at being a disciple but with the joy comes the wrestling to discover where I am meant to go and what I am meant to do. I am grateful to so many friends, older, wiser disciples and family, who helped me discern a calling to ordination. My struggle to discern any calling I may have had was in the context of so many questions and indeed frustrations with church and its relevance in my own community. However through my journey with Jesus I was becoming more aware of Jesus' command to 'Follow me', and that appeared to be leading to ordination. My confidence as a disciple was not in facts and certain knowledge, but 'It is the confidence of one who had heard and answered the call that comes from God through whom and for whom all things are made: "Follow me".' (Leslie Newbigin, *Proper Confidence: Faith, Doubt, and Certainty in Christian Discipleship*, p 105)

It was critical as I journeyed to have people to talk to, to pray with, to argue with, to struggle with and to laugh with. It was because other people discerned that I may be called that I started to probe this possibility. I certainly discovered how important we are to one another on this journey. Friends, and particularly soul friends, are such a blessing. They can help us feel faith when ours is struggling. They can on occasions carry us when we feel lost. They can be Jesus to us, and indeed we can be Jesus to them. It may appear as if I am shirking responsibility but I believe one of the reasons I was ordained was because of the conviction of others that affirmed me on this journey. Their confidence in me and in a calling for me, helped me believe despite the shadow of my struggle with church and despite the shadow of my own reluctance. The shadow of friends and family became a place where Jesus was able to drag me kicking and screaming towards ordination. In time, and with a wonderful experience at a selection conference for ordination training, I slowly came to believe that this is where I was meant to live out my discipleship.

I find great comfort in scripture when I read the stories of so many reluctant disciples who were not volunteering for service. There is the poignant struggle of Abram as he is called to be Abraham. The text describes it: 'Abraham fell face down; he laughed and said to himself, "Will a son be born to a man a hundred years old?"' (Genesis 17:17, *NIV*) Being called is something that demands humour, trust and obedience. There are no certainties and the future is open to all kinds of cul-de-sacs and maybe even wrong turns. The joy of this journey is that very uncertainty because, by its very nature, it leads to trust and peace. We do not know what lies ahead, but to discover we have to have faith and trust. Following Jesus is not some magic formula for success and well being. In fact, it is at times confusing, difficult but at the same time rewarding. However, this is where we

find peace and fulfilment. Faith itself is a paradox: we believe
but we do not know, we follow and we do not know where, but
as we do we find that image of God that is within us being restored as we become the people we are meant to be in him. In his
book, *The Challenge of Jesus*, Bishop Tom Wright describes this
vocation as follows: 'Humans are made in the image of God.
That is the equivalent, on the wider canvas, of Israel's position
and vocation. And bearing God's image is not just a fact, it is a
vocation. It means being called to reflect into the world the
creative and redemptive love of God.' (p 141)

What a profound, disturbing and exciting challenge for those
called to follow. From this call to follow Jesus came the call to
ordination but my reluctance was tangible. I was able to make
excuses based on my struggle with the institutional church, but
much deeper was my reluctance to have to live out my discipleship in such a public way. I certainly felt the reluctance of Jonah,
and I wanted to become a primary schoolteacher instead. That
plan never materialised and I found myself accepted for training and eventually ordained, with that reluctance still part of
my journey. This struggle was partly my lack of confidence that
I would have the patience and wisdom to fulfil the role.
Returning again to scripture, I find hope among the first disciples. They were a strange mix of humanity, an unusual collection of people and yet personally chosen. They were not volunteers – essentially they were conscripts. They were obviously
fascinated by Jesus but were constantly confused and unable to
understand what was happening. Even after Jesus' death they
were bewildered and it was sometime before they grasped the
enormity of what had happened. Bishop John Pritchard quotes a
spoof memorandum from the firm 'Jordan Management
Consultants', to Jesus, the would-be prophet at 'Joseph and Son,
General Builders, Nazareth':

Dear Sir:
Thank you for submitting the CVs of the 12 men you are considering for management positions in your new organisation.
All of them have taken our battery of tests and undergone
personal interviews with our psychologist and vocational
aptitude consultant. It is our opinion that most of your nom-

inees are lacking appropriate background, education and aptitude for the type of enterprise you are undertaking. Simon Peter is emotionally unstable and given to fits of temper. Andrew has no qualities of leadership. The two brothers James and John place personal interest above company loyalty. Thomas demonstrates a questioning mind that would tend to undermine morale. We feel it is our duty to tell you that Matthew has been blacklisted by the Jerusalem Better Business Bureau for possible fraud. James son of Alphaeus, and Thaddeus both show radical leanings and score highly on the manic-depressive scale. None of them seem inclined to team work.

There is, however, one candidate who shows potential. He is a man of ability and resourcefulness, has a keen business mind and is well connected. He is motivated, ambitious and can take responsibility. We recommend Judas Iscariot as your deputy and assistant and feel sure he would be an asset to your organisation. All the details are in the enclosed dossier.

We wish you every success in your new venture.' (*Living Jesus*, pp 34-35)

From this unusual group of disciples, the gospel spread quickly and very successfully. Their enthusiasm and energy is documented in scripture. They were convinced in the person of Jesus, they were transformed by their relational connection with him, not by a statement of faith and practice. Inspired and overwhelmed by the Holy Spirit, a unusual group of people did extraordinary things for God. That is exciting and it is what we are called to be. Their humanity and diversity gives me hope and belief. God can use me and you, and chooses to do so.

The call to ordination has led me to some unusual places. I have been privileged and blessed to meet some beautiful people and some of whom it was more difficult to believe that they were made in the image of God. The church would be easy if it were not for people. The difficulty is that all of us believe we are right and human nature seeks recognition and power. So many of the struggles are about power and dominant personalities. When I was struggling with this, a dear friend suggested I read the New Testament again and see if I could find the perfect church. I did and there isn't. Much of St Paul's writing's are about conflict and disputes. Even the great St Peter and St Paul had a major fall out. This following Jesus, particularly in church leadership, is fraught with tensions and struggles, but what a privilege to be called to bring Jesus to others.

As well as friends and family who helped me on my journey to ordination, there has been the shadow of encouragement in ministry that has helped me at those difficult times when, like Jonah, I wanted to do anything but follow. I have a series of scrapbooks that are a collection of letters and cards from those who have thanked me for helping them on their journey. These are a special gift of encouragement. I have always been an ad-mirer of Barnabas, 'son of encouragement, or of consolation'. He is one of the unsung heroes of the early church and his greatest gift was his Christ-like compassion and love, enabling him to encourage and support others, particularly Paul and the young John Mark. Encouragement is such an antidote to cynicism and despair. It is one of the most important gifts we can offer to each other and I have found it a shadow that has protected and strengthened me on my journey. It has helped affirm my calling and given me confidence in the gifts God has given me to exer-cise the ministry that is his and to which he has called me. They have been my 'shield of faith'. (Ephesians 6:16) When I have needed support and protection, they have stood with me and shielded me from losing hope.

One of the shadows that has disturbed me is that of cynicism. The church can be a place where cynicism can be so damaging. There is hurt, disillusionment, despair, falling numbers, low clergy morale, weariness at well doing and compassion fatigue. A cynic in the *Concise Oxford Dictionary* is defined as 'a person who has little faith in human sincerity and integrity'. Cynicism is like a slowly incoming tide – you can be unaware of, as it is en-veloping your thinking and indeed your actions. It is such a dangerous thought process for someone seeking to follow and reflect Jesus. He never gave up on people and paid the ultimate price of human rejection and scorn. In conversation with his rabbi, Mitch Albom recounts a conversation he had with him about cynicism. The rabbi is trying to explain that there is no place for cynicism and he uses the wonderful statement, 'If they spit in your face, you say it must be raining. But you still come back tomorrow.' (*Have a Little Faith*, p 47) It is not as easy as that might suggest, but it at least helps me recognise cynicism, and the need to not let it eat away at faith and hope.

The shadow of busyness and weariness can lead us to difficult places where cynicism and despair can easily take root. I speak from experience as someone who has always been busy doing and helping and have found myself exhausted emotionally, mentally and spiritually. We can believe that it is our responsibility to fix the problems in people, church and society. We are not called to *fix* but to *be*. There are so many distractions in ministry and unusual forms of stress. I will return to the subject of ministry in the next chapter but it is important to note, at this point, what it is we are called to. Walter Brueggemann in his book, *Mandate to Difference*, describes this struggle with great empathy:

> So what is it that makes people like us so weary? It is not the working too hard that makes us weary. It is rather, I submit, living a life that is against the grain of our true creatureliness, living a ministry that is against the true grain of our vocation, being placed in a false position so that our day-to-day operation requires us to contradict what we know best about ourselves and what we love most about our life as children of God. So consider this option. We are the weary ones whom Jesus invites in gentleness, because we are overly busy and overly anxious about the maintenance of our world. We are overly busy and overly anxious because we believe that one more pastoral call, one more committee meeting, one more careful preparation, one more published article, one more game of golf, one more staff review, one more check to make sure the lights are out and the dishes washed and the mail answered, one more anything will make this a better place and enhance our sense of self. (p 42)

There is the need for those of us who seek to follow Jesus to admit that this journey is difficult. That it is difficult standing as representatives for God in a world that is at times chaotic and full of pain that does not make sense. We need to be honest about our struggle in faith and admit to a broken world that we do not have the answers, but in faith we believe that together we can find hope in the chaos and peace in the pain. This is the gospel, the good news. It is not about making everything right but about finding God in the mess. That is the message of the baby lying in a manger. That was a dirty and smelly stable, with sheep dung and animal smells, a bloody placenta lying on the ground and the screams of childbirth. The first visitors were shepherds who were the riff-raff of society, a few strangers from the East and a choir of angels. We have sentimentalised and sanitised the amazing miracle of Bethlehem. God came into the mess, he didn't fix it.

As I continue this journey with Jesus as someone in leadership in the church, I want to rediscover the joy of *being* rather than *doing,* so as Jesus can carry me rather than me carry the burdens of the world which will only crush me. The words of Jesus are of critical importance for all who follow him.

> Are you tired? Worn out? Burned out on religion? Come to me. Get away with me and you'll recover your life. I'll show you how to take a real rest. Walk with me and work with me, watch how I do it. Learn the unforced rhythms of grace. I won't lay anything heavy or ill-fitting on you. Keep company with me and you'll learn to live freely and lightly.' (Matthew 11:28-30, The Message)

CHAPTER FIVE

Shadows of the Collar

'It's just that I had always felt that rabbis, priests, pastors, any cleric, really, lived on a plane between mortal ground and heavenly sky. God up there. Us down here. Them in between.' (Mitch Albom, *Have a Little Faith*, p 35) After thirty years in ordained ministry it is abundantly clear to me that people in parishes have many and varied expectations of those who are their ministers.

There are also the expectations and misunderstandings of those outside the church. In Susan Howatch's novel *Heartbreaker* one of the characters, Susanne, says: 'All I know about Christians is that they wear crosses with a man on them and do funny things on Sundays with a bloke that cross-dresses.' (p 344) In my lifetime in ministry there has been such a radical change in the perception and role of clergy. The church like any other public body has had its fair share of bad publicity and ridicule. There has been a massive shift in how people view the church, the faith and thereby those who are seen as their main representatives, the clergy. From my experience as a parish priest for more than twenty-five years, I understand that ordained ministry is a difficult and lonely task. However, I also know what an amazing privilege it is to be someone called to serve Jesus and thereby his church and the world. As someone who now has a particular responsibility for those who serve in ordained ministry, I want to acknowledge what a lonely and demanding role it can be. They face enormous challenges with little resources, an outdated structure and a church that is reluctant and hesitant about necessary change. I want to affirm them for their commitment and faith. John Drane in his book, *After McDonaldization*, writes: 'Christian ministry today, at least in the countries of the Global North, must be one of the toughest jobs on the planet, especially for those involved in leadership at the level of the local congregations.' (p 93)

It has been informative observing parishes as a bishop. They understandably want to ensure survival and even growth, but with as little change as possible. The expectation is that their rector will continue to operate parish life as it always has been and yet also be innovative enough not to upset too many. They will also be expected to bring in new members who will not be looking to change parish life. These are difficult tensions and are not made any easier by the lack of training in change management or vision setting, of previous generations of clergy. We have an archaic structure that stops us from doing so much that needs to be done. Clergy are so often maintaining structures of parish that are inadequate for mission and ministry in the twenty-first century. I will return to structures in a later chapter.

Our culture has also relegated church life and faith matters to the periphery of our society, and there is often ridicule and disdain heaped upon the clergy and church members. In Northern Ireland the Christian community feels under threat and that often leads to a defensive and insular approach to the wider community. There has to be a recognition by the churches that we deserve some of this mistrust and criticism.

There is a residual role for clergy in our society, but I believe we need to reflect on how the church has to change to be an agent of mission now. William Stringfellow, in reflecting upon the church in America, penned the following thoughts: 'The clergy have become hired spokespeople for religion in human life. They have been invited to decorate public life but restrained from intervening significantly in it. They have been relegated to the literal periphery – the invocations and the benedictions – of secular affairs.' (*A Private and Public Faith*, p 38)

There is a powerlessness in parish life to make the radical changes that are necessary, and that in turn can lead to huge frustrations and unresolved anger. 'There was a time, not too long ago, when we felt like captains running our own ships with a great sense of power and self-confidence. Now we are standing in the way. That is our lonely position: We are powerless, on the side, liked maybe by a few crew members who swab the decks and goof off to drink beer with us, but not taken very seriously when the weather is fine.' (Henri Nouwen, *The Wounded Healer*, p 88) The situation can be made more complex by some retired clergy announcing that all clergy have to do is what they did and visit people in their homes. There is the place for visiting but the society and culture we live in has changed so radically that simple solutions to our problems are not going to work. There is a failure to realise that the old models have been creaking for some time and should have been addressed sooner. The present generation of clergy have some very difficult journeys ahead but I also believe it is a very exciting time. It is increasingly obvious that we are, and will continue, to manage decline, unless the Holy Spirit transforms us and breathes new life within us. These tensions in parish life are clearly evident but we appear unwilling or unable to address them and that in turn creates even more angst and struggle for all the people of God.

With the difficulties for clergy, many are forced to find ways of coping and of seeking to have a ministry that can help them cope. Some find themselves becoming managers, others counsellors and others retreat into knocking doors and controlling people by the hardening of the 'oughteries'. Guilt is still a control mechanism that clergy can use to at least get people to turn up to church on a Sunday. Much of this struggle is carried out without adequate support structures and care for them, in an emotionally and spiritually draining environment. 'The unchallenged expectations of the "hierarchy", peers and congregations; changing expectations about status and authority in both church and society; a greater accountability, especially in professional conduct; negativity and suspicion in the press; past role models; new theories; the growing expectation that each priest will do more work; a high degree of mismatch between people and jobs; the desire of married clergy to take more part in the raising of their children and to be more creative in relating to their spouse; and perhaps most of all the demands they place upon themselves.' (Robin Greenwood, *Transforming Church*, p 30)

I am very conscious that one of the shadows for many clergy is that of loneliness. We have a hierarchical structure that makes care and support more difficult as the bishop, for example, can often be seen more akin to the school principal with his staff than a servant of the servants or a pastor to the pastors. There are so many burdens shared with those to whom pastoral care is offered and yet no supervision is organised by the church. The church should lead the way in caring for the carers. I do understand what compassion fatigue is like. I have sat in the place of the listener and felt that awful nagging knot in my gut that says I have nothing left to give to this person. I have dreaded the phone ringing to inform me of yet another death or pastoral crisis. I understand that it is easy to offer the public façade of coping, but of inwardly being in desperate need of help. To ask for help could be interpreted as not being able to cope.

I am writing these thoughts as a result of recognising that I had nothing left to give to others and I needed time to recover from years of giving. This is not about failure but about recognising that ordained ministry is very demanding especially if you are sensitive to the pain of others. 'The priest or pastor is constantly tempted to see himself as the answer-giver, the spiritual authority, the dispenser of grace and not its recipient.' (Philip Yancey, *Soul Survivor*, pp 289-90) Here there is another paradox that can be a shadow of darkness or of light. As ministers of the gospel of resurrection power and profound peace and joy, we often do not have that reality in our own lives because we have become exhausted helping others. We can be so busy serving others that we lose sight of our own needs and can assume that God will look after us without any help from us. We cannot help others unless we tend to our own needs and vulnerability. We are wounded healers – we too are in need of healing and grace as we also need the wonder of redemption.

One of the temptations of ordained ministry is to believe we are indispensable. We can easily find our worth and value in our role, rather than in being a cherished child of God. We can use our position to ensure we are needed and create a culture of dependency by default, thereby ensuring our role and purpose. Richard Rohr writes: 'The clergy often create a situation in which people need them so much, they can't live without them. I'm afraid some clergy – Catholic and Protestant – have done this to the people. For example, attendance at the service considered all-important. This overwhelming emphasis on social prayer has left many of our people passive, without a personal prayer life and comfortable with "handed-down-religion" instead of first-hand experience.' (*Everything Belongs*, p 147)

For anyone taking on the role of being rector in a Church of

Ireland parish, there is an outline of what is expected, in the Service of Institution and indeed in the Ordinal. However, these are based upon a model of church that essentially isn't in place anymore. We have a model of parish ministry designed for a church of times past, and not for the needs of the twenty-first century. Indeed, I was trained for a ministry that has changed beyond recognition even in the years I have been in parish life. These are real tensions and form one of the shadows that can make parish life more difficult. How do we minister to enable others to have their ministry? How do we ensure future growth and yet keep the traditionalists content? How do we ensure that we are engaging with the issues that concern local communities? These are genuine concerns for many in ordained ministry and yet the structures we operate under can make these questions difficult to respond to creatively. Clergy are often left to their own devices to decide how they want to develop parish life; some will consult with others, while others find it difficult to share responsibility and in fact they may think it is inappropriate. 'Many clergy are reacting violently against inherited patterns of assimilating the ministry of all, or acting in the place of Christ and allowing others to have a merely derived ministry, so that they offer nothing distinctive from Christian ministries. Others react, consciously and unconsciously, against recent attempts to transform understandings of priesthood, and disable others by holding on to all authority and decision-making. For example, the model of visiting consultant continues to be espoused by both clergy and bishops. Imagining that by ordination they are chosen and equipped to know what the whole reality of the church should be, such clergy take on the role of doctor to an ailing patient, the local church.' (Robin Greenwood, *Transforming Church*, p 29)

As well as these and other models of local church life, there is the added problem of people shopping around for a church that they prefer or a minister they like, rather than being involved in serving their local community through their local church. This is one of the many reasons why local churches are increasingly disconnected from local community and people.

In the midst of these shadows of parish life, there is the ordained person seeking to minister and make sense of ministry

today. There are many disillusioned people in ministry; they
may feel undervalued or misunderstood, either by those in authority over them or by their parishioners. Some are hanging on
until retirement, relieved that the future will be someone else's
problem. There are others who find alternative forms of ministry other than local church life. The church they trained for no
longer exists and the theological training they worked hard for
is no longer of value in exercising their ministry – in fact at times
it may appear to limit their ability to make the necessary
changes. There can be a real disempowerment in ministry for
many, and then there is a lack of further training and support. I
have observed these shadows as a parish priest and as a bishop.
I want to commend the many, many clergy who do such a wonderful job in such difficult circumstances, often without recognition, support or the necessary resources. In writing these thoughts
I want to stimulate reflection and discussion on the future structure and style of ministry and local church life. We need to give
those in ministry permission to take risks and to think and act
outside the box. 'Taking Jesus as our model for ministry could
be life-giving. In particular, we need to remember that Jesus always started where people were at, taking seriously their lived
experience (their stories), and then inviting them to see things in
the light of the bigger story of what God is doing. In our context,
this will involve opening up a space in which people can see
their own lives as the arena of God's activity, engaging in a con-
tinuous dialogue with scripture, and remaining the church in
the light of that experience.' (John Drane, *After McDonaldization*,
p 113)

One of the key issues that has been rediscovered in local
church life over the last number of decades has been the recognition of the ministry of all, and not just the clergy. A friend and
colleague, Bishop Richard Clarke, makes the following comments:

For centuries, the ordained ministry in the western traditions
has been understood in terms of power. Indeed the ordained
ministry was perceived as the summit of all Christian ministry, if not the totality of what was meant by ministry.
Gradually attitudes have changed and the term 'ministry of

the laity' has become more than a condescending formula for expecting greater effort and energy from the non-ordained members of the church. Unless the church as a whole thinks theologically with far more rigour (and it is the episcopal traditions which need to do the more major re-appraisals) about the nature of all ministry, it will lose heart and purpose. All ministry derives from God before it derives from church. It follows therefore that all ministry is of equal value and equal dignity. (*A Whisper of God*, p 43)

We tend to talk about the ministry of all, but in practice it appears to be more difficult to develop. It profoundly changes the role of the ordained clergy. Instead of being the person who does everything, they become the one who enables and equips others to do almost everything. This is becoming more urgent as the number of clergy reduces and the number of parish units without stipendiary clergy has increased. This also adds many more shadows for the clergy of volunteer management, delegation, team leadership and motivational skills. Many clergy have not been trained for this and it was not what they thought they were being ordained to do. These shadows will be different depending on how each individual clergy person reacts to the situation they find themselves in and on their own perception of ministry and theological understandings of church and ministry.

There are serious questions for us to address in the future development of ministry and some of these are being addressed in the new model of ordination training taking place in The Church of Ireland Institute. That is an exciting development for the wider church. However, I have a concern that we will give vision and fresh impetus to those called to serve in the ordained ministry but we haven't addressed the serious issue that parishes may not be willing to accept fresh thinking and innovative developments in parish life and ministry. 'Our theology of ordination and the symbols that support it simply have not kept pace with the Holy Spirit's leading in the church. What is needed is an understanding of ordination that is catholic without being authoritarian and that views leadership not as something separate or distinct from the community of faith, but as something that is affirmed and empowered from within. The ordained person is not someone set apart, but someone set within the community of faith as a sign of what we are called to be. As we approach the twenty first-century we are being asked to think in new ways about who we are in relation to one another. We are being asked to listen to voices in our midst that we have not heard before.' (James Fenhagen, in *Shaping the Future* edited by Stephen Freeman, pp 79-80)

These shadows of ministry are complex and yet critical for the future life of Christ's ministry and Christ's church. My experience as parish priest and bishop give me hope, as I have met and know many of Christ's disciples who are willing to follow where he leads us. There is need for structural change and for a willingness to take risks and give permission for experiment and a messy model of church life, that doesn't fit into our present structures.

My granny taught me when I was a child the importance of the carrot and the stick. There was usually a reward given for some chore that had to be done – the carrot helped the pain of the stick. Although my granny also had a phrase that as a child I never quite understood. After helping her in some manner, with a twinkle in her eye, she would say: 'You'll never see what I'll buy you.' When it comes to reflecting on the shadows that I have outlined in connection with parish ministry I believe there is a metaphorical carrot and stick. If we do not address these issues and find new models of ministry and church, we will continue to decline. If we do seek to discover new models with the leading of the Holy Spirit, we are guaranteed an exciting future even though we do not know where that will lead us.

I conclude this chapter with a prayer from the Covenant Service of the Methodist Church;

I am no longer my own but yours.
Put me to what you will,
rank me with whom you will;
put me to doing, put me to suffering;
let me be employed for you or laid aside for you,
exalted for you or brought low for you;
let me be full, let me be empty,
let me have all things, let me have nothing;

I freely and wholeheartedly yield all things
to your pleasure and disposal.
(Methodist Covenant Service in *The Methodist Worship Book*,
p 290)

CHAPTER SIX

The Phone Call

I will never forget the phone ringing that day. From that moment everything changed and life would never be the same again. It had been a normal Tuesday morning, staff meeting with the usual craic and work. The week ahead planned and that great sense of belonging to each other, of affirmation and support. It was Tuesday 17 April, a week after the celebration of Easter and the week after the celebrations in Glasgow of a special birthday. The sandwich had just been eaten and I was preparing to go and visit in one of the local hospitals, when the phone rang.

Let me explain some of the background that led to this moment. In the Church of Ireland bishops are elected by an electoral college. Chapter 6, Part 1, point 4, of the Church of Ireland Constitution describes what this is.

> An Episcopal Electoral college shall consist of:
> (a) the President of the College, who shall be the archbishop of the province which includes the diocese of which the see is vacant ...
> (b) three members of the House of Bishops nominated by that House;
> (c) twelve diocesan clerical and twelve diocesan lay Episcopal electors from the diocese of which the see is vacant;
> (d) (i) when the diocese of which the see is vacant is situated in the province of Armagh, two diocesan clerical, two diocesan lay Episcopal electors from each of the other dioceses in the province;

When the electoral college meets, various candidates are discussed and votes cast. For anyone to be elected a bishop they have to receive two-thirds of the votes from both the clergy and lay votes. The electoral college to elect a bishop for the diocese of

Connor met in March and no candidate received the necessary majority and when this happens the decision goes back to the House of Bishops to choose someone. They met on 17 April, the day I received the phone call.

I had not been a candidate at the electoral college and had not been asked would I be willing to be considered and I am glad I wasn't. I had no time to worry about what might be. So the phone call came without warning and when I answered the phone in the rectory kitchen I was not expecting to hear the voice of Archbishop Alan Harper. I can remember the conversation verbatim. He said the following: 'We have just finished a meeting of the House of Bishops and it seems good to us and the Holy Spirit to appoint you Bishop of Connor.' After a long pause as my mind was in turmoil, he then asked me: 'Are you alright?' I will never forget my reply: 'I am wondering if I can say no to that?' That was taken as a yes and he then quickly explained what would happen next, as it would be announced publicly in the next thirty minutes. He also suggested that I should have some thoughts on what my priorities would be as bishop. I put the phone down and then began to wonder had I dreamt this or was it really happening. I was in shock. However, very quickly I received a message of encouragement from my own bishop and realised this was actually happening. I immediately rang my family, colleagues and close friends. The house and phone were very busy for the rest of the day and it was all somewhat of a blur.

I do remember thinking about what the archbishop had said about priorities and immediately knew what my number one would be. I wanted to be a pastor to the pastors and I still do. This is critical because of the level of care that they offer to others and the burdens that they carry with no formal or organised supervision or support. Ministry in today's church is a lonely and at times thankless task. I believe we need to show our appreciation to those who try their best in very difficult circumstances. It is easy to criticise and complain but I know from experience that the one negative comment is remembered much more than the one hundred positives.

The following weeks and months are difficult to remember. Much of the time was spent saying goodbye to so many people.

After over seventeen years in Ballyholme, we weren't saying goodbye to parishioners, but people who had become part of our lives, who helped shape us and mould us in so many ways. It is only with hindsight that I can recognise that I was in shock for months and also suffering from the grief of leaving such a community of support and friendship. We also left our family home where our two children had grown up and we had been blessed in so many ways. Within eight weeks of the phonecall, we had moved house and shortly after I was ordained a bishop on St Peter's Day, 29 June.

I found the words of Anne Lewin's poem called 'Stage fright', helpful:

> It's often somewhat
> Disconcerting when
> God takes at our word.
> 'Take me and use me',
> We say, meaning it; But when God does,
> There is a moment of surprise,
> Perhaps terror, 'Me?'

> Then our 'Yes' loved from us,
> Comes the realisation
> That the opportunity is gift,
> The outcome held in grace.
> (*Watching for the Kingfisher*, p 1)

There was little time to catch my breath and I suddenly realised that there were more than a few tasks waiting for me and a huge expectation that I would know what a bishop needed to do and I would just do it. I found myself in various meetings and looking around when someone would say 'bishop'. It was such a shock that I was now in the place that I had watched others in for a few decades. There were moments when I found it difficult to adjust to this new office and role. In worldly terms I had made it, I was the 'boss' and yet in the life of following Jesus this left me struggling with what appeared to be contradictions. A bishop, above all else, is a servant of the servants. Phillip Yancey expresses the essence of this helpfully: 'The great paradox which scripture reveals to us is that real and total freedom can only be found through downward mobility. The Word of God came down to us and lived among us as a slave. The divine way is indeed the downward way.' (*Soul Survivor*, p 298) I think it is unusual but nonetheless standard practice in our tradition that clergy are appointed to senior posts and are expected to do the job, without a job description or further training and preparation. I know that for any bishop there is the ordinal that outlines what is expected in general terms. However, it is clear to me from my new perspective that every diocesan bishop has to work that out differently, because the task is so deeply influenced by each and every different diocesan context.

I also found myself struggling with a shadow that had. always been difficult for me, but it now became more focused. One of the things I have always sought to do is be myself in ministry and not perform a role that made me be someone different. As a bishop this has been more difficult, because people do have expectations of bishops and most people treat them with a certain diffidence. Clergy are not quite sure how to treat you, as you are the 'boss', and very often people in parishes want to bend your ear and assume you have the power to do anything and the answer to all the difficult situations. Penny Jamieson describes this shadow in a way that made me smile: 'I scarcely knew myself during those first few months, years even, and neither did other people. I began to be called by titles and names that sat awkwardly with me ... This came to me in particular incidents which acted as vignettes on how others saw me. One most startling occurred when I met a lay person in the supermarket: 'Do bishops have to shop too?' ... There was a tension, for, like it or not, I was a bishop, and that fact was bound to affect all my contacts with others.' (*Living at the Edge*, pp 167-68)

I found myself reading and asking questions about *episcope* in scripture and tradition. I discovered three themes emerged. The bishop is seen as a focus for the unity of God's people. There is also the important theme of enabling, developing and sustaining the ministry of others. To keep watch over the ministry of others and the parishes in the diocese and, not to be forgotten, one's own ministry. A task that certainly was daunting as I readjusted from the cut and thrust of parish life to the oversight that I was now responsible for. 'The Greek word *episcope* simply means watching over. In the Septuagint, the Greek Old Testament, the word also carries the meaning to visit. We should have in mind therefore a proactive, protective, missional watching over, not the role of a passive spectator. *Episcope* is not to be simply a stewardship of existing resources and congregations but a dynamic seeking of new opportunities for mission and the establishing of new communities.' (*The Future of the Parish System*, edited by Steven Croft, pp 86-7)

There were new shadows forming in this new role and office. This is undoubtedly a more isolating ministry and I certainly found a massive gap in not belonging to a local community, particularly as I had been given so much affirmation in the local context. I am in a different parish every Sunday and that has taken some time to get used to. Even though in our ecclesiology, as Anglicans, we state that the parish is the responsibility of the bishop and the rector, I still felt like the visiting preacher. I am very grateful for the warmth of the welcome I have received but it was still a shadow that I had lost so much in leaving the security of the parish, where I had been blessed to be for so many years.

I also became aware very quickly of the enormity of the task in overseeing the diocese as we sought to look for growth in a context of decline and where many parishes are struggling to keep their finances in a healthy state. In my lifetime the City of Belfast has changed beyond recognition and parish life in general has been very stressful for many and varied reasons. There is a deep disconnection between the local churches and local communities. People are questioning the value of church and indeed the reality of what we teach and preach. There has at times been an over saturation with a narrow definition of gospel that only talked about the afterlife and sin. There still is a huge task ahead and I want to challenge every parish to dream dreams and find new ways of connecting with people in the local community where the parish is based.

I have been asked what is the big difference between being a rector and being a bishop. The best analogy I can find to explain the difference is that as rector of a large parish I was captain of a large ferry, as bishop I feel as if I am captain of the *Titanic*. I use the *Titanic* deliberately because somehow as God's people in parish and diocese we need to find new directions to avoid the iceberg of decline and despair. Brian McLaren writes a word of encouragement: 'Episcopalians, Lutherans, Methodists and others with bishops can use the episcopacy to turn around their ocean liner.' (*A New Kind of Christianity*, p 217)

There have been other shadows in being a bishop. It is an issue that I have discussed with other bishops and there is no easy answer. One of the responsibilities of a bishop is for the care of the clergy, as pastor to the pastors, something I believe is of critical importance. However, there are times when the interests of clergy and people are diametrically opposite and the bishop is responsible for the mission and witness of the whole church. This is a shadow I have to learn to live with and pray for wisdom and grace, recognising there are times I cannot fix it. Penny Jamieson expresses this concern when she writes: 'The pastoral responsibility of the bishop is for the health and Christian integrity of the whole church. It clearly is a responsibility that can clash with the one-to-one responsibility for the welfare of individual clergy.' (*Living at the Edge*, p 66)

There is also the tension between the pastoral role and the judicial, in upholding the Constitution of the church with someone with whom I have a pastoral relationship. There are those who will argue that the judicial role is so important that it is almost impossible for the bishop to act pastorally. I find this a shadow that causes me heartache as I seek to uphold the rule book but also offer important pastoral care to those who give so much. I will always believe and seek to practise the wonder of grace in and through Jesus.

The response of so many people to leadership has been a shadow of light and hope. I believe there are those who are looking for vision and direction, but offered with care and sensitivity. Yet at the same time there is a shadow in this context that brings some discomfort. Robin Greenwood expresses this thoughtfully: 'At all levels of church activity, still pervaded by the expectation of respectful subordination, we are often inhibited from creatively and honestly offering appropriate critique to senior figures. Why do we still want to lie at the feet of leaders who are above contradiction, only to reject them when they cannot meet our every expectation?' (*Transforming Church*, p 17)

My experience as a rector taught me many things about vision, change, strategies and people. One of the great dangers in church life is that we can become programme-driven, losing sight of what is at the heart of church and that is community and relationship. Dietrich Bonhoeffer apparently once said:

> He who loves his dream of the Christian community more than the Christian community itself becomes a destroyer of the latter, even though his personal intentions may be ever so honest and earnest and sacrificial.

Throughout my journey with Jesus and ordained ministry, I have been very conscious of the words from St John's gospel: 'You did not choose me but I chose you.' (John 15:16a). I have struggled with the call to ordained ministry but I cannot deny that it is where I believe I am meant to be. This has always been a shadow for me. Sometimes in the difficult moments I have wanted to leave the ordained ministry, but I know I would not be at peace if I did. There are times my reluctance has made it difficult for me to live at ease with the calling. I can hear my granny say: 'Gurn up and get on with it!' I have made the journey more difficult by my reluctance and my struggle with the call. Although I believe it has also helped me understand and empathise with so many people that find church a difficult place. This shadow is another paradox that is part of the journey and it is why I find the words of Jesus in St John's gospel so affirming. Laurence Freeman reflects on Jesus choosing the disciples in the following way: 'The gospels show that Jesus did not select his disciples because they were virtuous or wise. Jesus chose his disciples, they did not choose him, for reasons best known to himself, and he accepted them as they were.' (*Jesus the Teacher Within*, p 215) When I now interview those considering a possible call to ordination, I find that reluctance is usually a helpful part of their call.

In the weeks before my ordination as bishop, I managed to spend some days in the Benedictine Monastery in Rostrevor. The hospitality is a wonderful and affirming gift and the food is excellent! The rhythm of the worship is restful and allows for contemplation and reflection. I also managed to spend some time talking to Dom Mark-Ephrem Nolan about my journey.

During those few days I found myself facing so many internal
fears that haunted me. As I walked, talked and listened I was beginning to realise the enormity of the task to which I had been
called, and hence the fear. Fear has always been a shadow on
my journey. I am sure it relates to my childhood. I am at my
most vulnerable when things are going well, as I start to look for
the disaster waiting to happen. As a child of six, losing my dad
left me feeling very vulnerable to good times because inevitably
that is when trouble will come. My appointment had led to so
many good wishes and very kind things being said about me,
that left me feeling vulnerable.

In conversation Brother Mark gave me some insights and
walked with me, listening, with an amazing gift of insight and
clarity for which I am very grateful. I was also struggling with
this new role and how I was now to be treated differently and it
would lead me to some new and difficult places. One of the
phrases he shared with me was that he said I should remain
'holy indifferent'. Indifferent to the deference and place of respect I would have as a bishop, not in any way to lessen respect
for the office of bishop, but to ensure I didn't start to believe that
this change was about me. I could easily find myself believing
that I was a very important person and lose the recognition that
I am a disciple of Jesus who is a wounded healer, dependent on
his grace for everything. Hence the holy, of 'holy indifference':
my main task was to keep my focus on being a disciple and staying close to Jesus. It was from him that I received the calling and
from him I would receive the grace and strength to fulfil the calling. Henri Nouwen's words are very helpful: 'It almost seems as
if they are necessary reminders of your need to stay close – very
close – to Jesus. Jesus is where you are and you can trust that he
will show you the next step.' (*The Inner Voice of Love*, p 16)

That is still my prayer and I ask others to pray this for me, because it is in Jesus that I can fulfil the calling that I still find very
demanding, and also an enormous privilege. There is an interesting and at times difficult journey ahead because leadership is
fraught with tensions and opportunities. In the book edited by
Steven Croft, *The Future of the Parish System*, the Bishop of
Peterborough, Ian Cundy, sets out the role of the bishop in a
way that I find inspiring and focused. I finish this chapter with

the hope and prayer that this may be true for all who have been called to Episcopal ministry and diocesan leadership in today's church.

It is the role of the bishop and his staff who have the 'oversight' of the diocese and see the big picture, to ask how the mission of the church is to be maintained in the present circumstances and with the resources available. The mission of God is central to its purpose and must flow organically from its worship. As a bishop I feel committed to the task, with the help of my colleagues, of maintaining and developing an effective, outward-looking, worshipping Christian presence in every community throughout the diocese, and developing such an effective presence in each new development and network. It is demanding task, but that is where our focus should be. (p 164)

CHAPTER SEVEN

Perspectives?

One of my special memories from my childhood was holidays with my grandparents, auntie, uncle and cousins in a holiday home on the coast outside Donaghadee. I enjoyed watching my grandfather sitting on a summer evening looking at the various ships sailing up and down Belfast Lough through his binoculars. He received so much pleasure from recounting where each ship was going to or coming from. The binoculars gave him such a wonderful view and, of course, we would be encouraged to look through them and gain that perspective.

Over the years I have been challenged to gain a healthier perspective on the church. I don't mean the denomination I belong to but to the institution of church. I would have wanted to argue that I had a healthy disrespect for the church, but I think I was wanting to excuse my negative thinking. As I reflect upon scripture and history I see clearly yet another paradox that is important to acknowledge. The church is the Body of Christ in the world and as such is special and unique. It is called by God to be the bearer in word and deed of the good news of God's amazing grace. It is called and equipped for this purpose. However, it is also a human institution with all it's dreadful mistakes and power struggles. Historically it has a track record in some areas that should cause shame, and some areas that should cause celebration.

I may have concentrated too much on the failings and thereby almost denied my calling not to fix it but to play my part. It is easy to be critical and negative but that denies what God has called us to in Christ, to be members with each other in his body and to incarnate the presence of Jesus in the mess of the world.

Archbishop Michael Ramsey observed the following: 'When therefore we say that we believe in the church, we do so only in terms of our belief in the God who judges and raises up. The mistake of ecclesiasticism through the ages has been to believe in the church as a kind of thing-in-itself. The apostles never regarded the church as a kind of thing-in -itself. Their faith was in God, who had raised Jesus from the dead, and they knew the power of his resurrection to be at work in them and their fellow-believers, despite the unworthiness of them all.' (A. M. Ramsey and Leon-Joseph Suenens, *The Future of the Christian Church*)

As Christians we need to recognise the failings of the church throughout the centuries but we also need to recognise that in Christ we are part of the story. We have an awesome responsibility and privilege to be the church in our generation. Dorothy Day explains this tension as follows: 'As to the church, where else shall we go, except to the bride of Christ, one flesh with Christ? Though she is a harlot at times, she is our Mother. We should read the book of Hosea, which is a picture of God's steadfast love not only for the Jews, his chosen people, but for his church, of which we are every one of us members or potential members.' (*Dorothy Day Selected Writings* edited by Robert Ellsberg, p 339) The church is called to be an agent of God's mission in the world; in each and every generation and culture that is it's calling. Jürgen Moltmann articulates this principle: 'It is not the church that has a mission of salvation to fulfil in the world, it is the mission of the Son and the Spirit through the Father that includes the church' (*The Church in the Power of the Spirit*, p 64)

The beginnings of the church in scripture is a fascinating account of ordinary people making an extraordinary difference to world history and culture. In the record as we have it, particularly in *The Acts of the Apostles*, there are certain things that stand out as core values. 'Acts 2:42 is often regarded as laying down 'the four marks of the church'. The apostles' teaching; the common life of those who believed; the breaking of the bread and the prayers. These four go together. You can't separate them, or leave one out, without damage to the whole thing.' (*Acts for Everyone Part 1*, N. T. Wright, p 44)

As I reflect on these strands I can see them as shadows for light and darkness on my journey. I am very grateful to those who have taught me and equipped me as I seek to live out my discipleship. There were those who taught me when I was ques-

tioning and struggling to make sense of faith in my teenage
years. The people who I remember are those who were patient
and allowed me to question and probe. It was not just what they
said but how they lived their answers, and also that they sometimes admitted they didn't know the answers. It strikes me when
I read the gospels that Jesus taught the first disciples by modelling what he taught. He didn't give them words but a lifestyle, in
how he related to people, in how he dealt with the outcasts and
rejected, by how he included women and valued them, in how
he dealt with conflict and raged at hypocrisy and injustice. This
teaching was three dimensional and exuded integrity.

There are friends who have taught me new lessons in faith as
they shared their story with me and enabled me to be challenged and encouraged me by their experience and learning.
Some have even helped me realise I am not always right, and
that is not just my family! The gift of fellow travellers is a God-
given gift and I have found them to be a shadow of light and
strength on the journey.

The apostles' teaching is not always about sermons, as it
maybe interpreted by some. I do believe passionately in the importance and value of sermons but we do not learn solely by
head knowledge. John Pritchard comments on preaching with a
delightful wit: 'I notice that a national newspaper said that a
survey had shown that sermons were getting shorter and went
on to suggest: "This is an impressive testimony to the power of
intercessory prayer".' (*The Life and Work of a Priest*, p 33)

I believe that preaching is vital for the worshipping community, but I also believe that we have made the mistake of seeing
preaching as the only way of teaching the faith. The arguments
have then been about the length of sermons and how scripture
is used or abused. We have in general failed, as churches, to cat-
echise people in discipleship. People do not learn adequately
from sermons, but we need to be taught as we reflect upon our
lives, scripture and teaching. I have received much from sermons but I have learnt so much more from reflecting, reading,
discussing and observing others live the faith. Recently our
adult children, who are students, have challenged me by how
they live with simplicity, generosity and a genuine concern for
those who are in need.

The other side of this shadow has been some of the teaching which has been harsh, judgemental and lacking in grace. In our culture we have those who want to teach exclusion, self-right-eousness and control by guilt. I have also been disturbed by the way in which many churches are focused on numbers of people attending rather than by the need to equip people for disciple-ship. We need to help develop communities of disciples who will live out the faith in their towns, streets and countryside, who will not have to spend all their time and energy keeping the local structure of church afloat.

In his book, *Transforming Church*, Robin Greenwood gives the following analysis that I find disturbing but insightful: 'We continue to work with language, concepts and practices that together create representative pictures of the identity of God, religion, ministry and church that are self-limiting. One notable example is our persistent rootedness in a doctrine of individual-ism, dominated by incipient clerical control of the Christian community. Another is to place ourselves beyond the compre-hension of most ordinary human life and agendas. In particular I have in mind those aspects of local church assumptions and practice that deliberately displace the work of the people of God by clergy and bishops as though this were a fundamental gospel truth; place emphasis on the solitary individual finding salva-tion and the assurance of God's love in isolation; make only reluctant connections between the experience of worship and everyday responsibilities; fail to support people in the diversity of their everyday working roles; are inward-looking or claim to read God's word exclusively from the Bible; ignore the complex-ity of life in the world now by working in step-by-step linear ways; separate the life of the church from complex contempo-rary pointers about leadership and management; and cut them-selves off from churches that take different perspectives.' (p 41) There is an enormous challenge for twenty-first century disci-ples who are the church, and I am glad that it is God the Holy Spirit that teaches us, leads us and can transform us.

When I spend time in the Benedictine monastery in Rostrevor, I see clearly the richness and strength of community, when a group of people have committed to Jesus and to each other, to live out their faith for the good of others. That commu-

nity is such a blessing to so many by their hospitality, acceptance, prayer, worship and joy. I have experienced different communities throughout my journey and they have been a shadow
of warmth and support, radiating the grace of God in tangible
ways. In the different parishes I have been privileged to serve
there has always been a community of people who have shared
their lives with me and enriched me and my family by giving of
themselves to us. I was overwhelmed by the love and support of
people in Ballyholme Parish when my mother died: they gave
us as a family so much support, they exhibited the presence of
Jesus to us in many different ways, from food to presence and
understanding. After the famous phone call they also enveloped
us in affirmation and love, making the parting easier than it
might have been. This community life is a wonderful gift and a
testimony to the love and grace of the one we seek to serve. John
Pritchard makes the following observation: 'The church has
been "doing community" for a very long time and knows a
thing or two that governments have been trying to discover for
decades.' (*Living Jesus*, p 132)

In reflecting upon the gospel narrative, it is fascinating to ob-
serve Jesus forming a new community. There was a clear message of forgiveness of sins, underpinned by the command to
love one another. This community supported Jesus as he revealed the kingdom of God through acts of loving service. They
withdrew together, they ate together. Meals form a major part of
their story and they shared years of their lives with each other.
Steven Croft articulates the need for 'transforming communities' today where there is 'depth of friendship and relationship;
discipleship within structures of mutual accountability; worship and prayer which arise from and are closely related to shared
lives; and a common sense of persons enabling one another to
share in the mission of God.' (*Transforming Communities*, p 72)
There is a rich foundation of communities throughout our
churches, but there is still much to be facilitated to enable us to
do so much more, not least on an ecumenical basis that puts
kingdom before denomination.

It is observing the battles between various communities that
claim to be following Jesus where I have found this core value to
be a dark shadow. There is something in the human psyche that

wants to compete and finds it very hard to share or rejoice when others appear to be enjoying new life and growth. That competitive spirit is not something that reflects well on the God we claim to represent and serve. I have also observed communities that can tear themselves apart with misunderstanding and power struggles. Conflict in churches appears to be vicious, and grace can find no home there. These are dark shadows and often happen when we lose sight of why we are there in the first place, and it is not our agenda that matters but the glory of God and the declaration by word and deed of his amazing love. Our communities of faith or local churches, and indeed national churches, must not become an end in themselves, as they are there to serve the purposes of God and not human agendas. 'The true community of Jesus Christ does not rest in itself. It does not merely contemplate the striving of the world with its better knowledge. It does not refrain from active participation. It exists as it actively reaches beyond itself into the world.' (*Theological Foundations for Ministry*, edited by R. S. Anderson, p 514)

It is fascinating that those who journeyed on the Emmaus road eventually recognised Jesus when they broke bread together. A wonderful Eucharistic moment that they would never forget. My early experience of the breaking of bread was to watch hundreds of people leave church after morning prayer when the holy communion would be added on at the end, when a handful of people would stay. I couldn't understand then why people would leave and, with my experience since, it makes even less sense now. In the Protestant culture that I inherited from my faith community, there appeared to be a nervousness about receiving communion – only the very holy should receive. This was never stated but it was assumed. There was also an unspoken concern that it was only Roman Catholics that took communion on even a daily basis. Over the years I have come to value the wonder and joy of celebrating the Eucharist. Jesus is present with his people in the bread and wine. I do not want to define that which is a mystery but enjoy the beauty of God's presence. This act of worship contains the critical elements of worship for any disciple: 'We hear again in the words of the service and especially in the words of scripture, God's call to come and follow and to be part of this new community. We are invited to share together in the body and blood of Christ present through faith in the bread and wine; an effective sign both of the death and res-urrection of Christ for our sake, but also of our own intimate communion with God and his presence in the life of the believ-er.' (*Transforming Communities*, Steven Croft, p 118)

The Eucharist has become such a vitally important source of grace for me on the journey, a shadow of wonderful joy and strength. However, it also casts a shadow over my journey as I cannot receive this sign of unity with some of my fellow pil-grims – that is a deep and painful reminder of our brokenness as the body of Christ. It is profoundly sad that we can divide that which God has declared one in him.

It has to be one of the great struggles on the journey of faith. I have spoken to so many people over the years that do it but find it difficult and I can identify with them. Prayer has been a painful and joyful struggle of discovery. There is no magic for-mula or easy guidebook to follow. Everybody who seeks to fol-low Jesus finds prayer difficult.

The essence of our discipleship is relationship, and hence the importance of prayer. To Clement of Alexandria is attributed the saying: 'Prayer is keeping company with God.' In this rela-tionship it is God who has taken the initiative, prayer begins in heaven not on earth. It is a wonderful grace gift. Prayer formed a dark shadow in my youth as I always thought it was some-thing I had to do. It was such an effort. I had to do it out of duty and it appeared to me as if I was talking to myself. Once I began to recognise that prayer begins with God's love for me, and prayer is my response to that love, it allowed me to experiment and even to fail. I found myself being honest with God and ex-pressing my struggle and even my anger. Prayer over the years is still a struggle, but it is much more about resting in God's presence than a burden. It has become more of a response of love rather than of a duty.

To discover that prayer is about receiving God's forgiveness and unconditional love has been a wonderful shadow of divine presence. Being in God's presence gives God the potential to change me, to be transformed by his friendship. Archbishop Michael Ramsey wrote: 'To be with God wondering, that is ador-ation. To be with God gratefully, that is thanksgiving. To be with God ashamed, that is contrition. To be with God with others on the heart, that is intercession.' (*Be Still and Know*, p 74) Prayer is being with God and God is with us always. In prayer we can discover that God is always seeking us.

Praying in public has been a more difficult shadow. I have always found it difficult. How do you lead so many others in prayer when they must be thinking their own thoughts and prayers? There are people I have the joy of sharing ministry with who have a gift for leading public prayer and it is something we need to encourage and give permission for, to ensure that others are given their place within the body of Christ. I have found using music and even simple choral responses can help the context and value of corporate prayer. Within the Church of Ireland it has not always been the custom for informal prayer meetings and many people are terrified by such gatherings. As an introvert, I never found them easy and I have been concerned they were a place where some people used to flaunt their self-righteousness. Yet it is important that we are comfortable in any place to be able to pray, recognising that it is keeping company with God. It is good to take time to do that together. 'We need the inspiration of the Spirit; we need to speak about God as people who have seen the invisible. It can only happen when we learn to pray. We must appreciate and understand the value of prayer in our lives; parishes must become schools of prayer; families should build their unity on prayer together; our lay organisations will only limp along unless they help their members to pray more intensely. Whenever we come together for meetings, we should always spend some time praying together. I would not be happy if that meant only saying formal prayers together.' (*To be a Pilgrim*, Cardinal Basil Hume, p 48)

On this journey with Jesus, the church has brought me such support and grace but it has also brought me pain and struggle. It is cherished and loved by God but its members are fallible human beings in need of God's grace and healing. I am one such pilgrim and recognise my own brokenness. As I continue to struggle with the church, I also recognise that God has called the church and given her a special role within the mission of God. If God has called, we believe that God will equip and use, despite any failings of broken humanity. I find the words of Brian

McLaren sum up my hope and prayers for the church I am a member of: 'I love churches. Of course, I've seen enough churches at close enough range for long enough that I'm not naïve about them, nor am I unaware of their serious problems and dysfunctions. But I believe in "one, holy, catholic and apostolic church", as the old creed says, and in the holy faith with which she is entrusted. And I believe that, like Sarah and Elizabeth, just when you think the old girl is over the hill, she will take a pregnancy test and surprise us all.' (*A New Kind of Christian*, preface page xi.)

CHAPTER EIGHT

I Have a Dream ... But!

One of the difficulties in church life is being able to question what we do without appearing over-critical at a time when the church is being sidelined and criticised by so many voices. However, before we dream dreams there has to be a recognition of the context. The two quotes that follow are by people who are very concerned about the future but who are looking at the reality of that context.

> Church is what some others do. It is noticed sadly, in their terms, not only as an alien and an expensive building, that I wouldn't know what to do in, worse, it is occupied by people I wouldn't want to be seen dead with.' (George Lings, *Living Proof – a new way of being church*, Church Army 1999, p 13)

> The church is perceived as just one more thing that – whatever its usefulness to previous generations – is now well and truly past its sell-by date.' (John Drane, *After McDonaldization*, p 13)

I believe in the church and recognise that the church is the 'Body of Christ' and that it is called to be an integral part of God's mission. Yet I am also concerned that, having served for thirty years in the Church of Ireland, we have structures and traditions that are hampering us in that mission rather than enabling it. Hence, I have a dream. I do not have any blueprint for change but I have reflections, comments and suggestions to make as I articulate that dream. My hope and prayer is that we can emerge from some of the shadows that block the light to find new shadows that liberate and enable.

In reflecting upon my experiences as an ordained minister there are so many lessons that I have learnt, and indeed mistakes I have made, but some of the shadows that haunted me were not of my own making. I was ordained into a church that

valued and values those who are ordained, and over decades
they have been given a privileged place in people's lives. They
are welcomed into homes, invited to share in the joy and pain of
people's lives, given authority to administer the sacraments and
guide parishes as they seek to live out the faith. The changes in
our culture, lifestyle and even in church, is staggering. My first
computer that I bought in the late 80s would now be considered
archaic by my adult children. The speed of change is rapid and
technology is constantly being updated and the latest gadget is
quickly superseded by a newer model. Within my lifetime in ordained ministry, the Church of Ireland has had two new prayer
books and various temporary ones, two new hymn books, voted
in favour of the ordination of women and has twice put major
changes in place for ordination training. These changes haven't
been without real internal tensions and pain. However, the way
parishes function has not changed. Added to this, people in
parishes have become more demanding of their clergy and more
willing to express their frustrations. In our religious culture, my
experience is that religious people are sometimes the most difficult, as they are always right and at times appear to have a hot-
line to heaven.

After twenty years as rector in two different parishes, it is
obvious to me that the structure and expectations of parishes
made changes in parish life difficult to implement. I found myself trying to maintain the essence of parish life that was gener-
ally expected and, at the same time, gently trying to help the
parish engage with the local community and with those who
didn't belong. It was an exercise in juggling, to maintain the old
and at the same time make the changes that were necessary, to
help the church do what it was called to do and that is to incarnate the presence of Jesus. 'The word "parish" is never used in the
New Testament, but it is, interestingly, an ancient Greek word,
which literally means "those outside the house": not the insid-
ers, but the outsiders. So a parish church, in an ideal world, is
not an exclusive place, but an inclusive place for the local
stranger; for those who don't know the way, the truth and the
life; for those who don't know they have a place in the heart of
God, and who are ignorant of their own reservation in heaven. It
is the insider place for the outsider; the only club that exists for

non-members, as William Temple once quipped.' (*The Future of the Parish System*, edited by Steven Croft, p 4)

These tensions were more complex and subtle because the parishes, in the diocese in which I served all my ministry, as curate and rector, paid the stipend. Within the context of managing change and trying to develop new ideas, this became more difficult because I was dependent on their support to pay the bills. For many parishes, money is a real concern and sadly much of the income pays the stipend and the upkeep of buildings that are very expensive to maintain and keep in good repair. 'Looking after magnificent historic buildings for their own sake is not a central aim of the churches. The *raison d'être* of church buildings is to provide places for Christian worship.' (*Strategic Church Leadership*, R. Gill and D. Burke, p 88)

Parishes are also becoming more difficult to sustain because of lack of finances. Many parishes are becoming more dependent upon an ageing population who have been very generous, but who are now living on pensions and thus lower income that means giving is decreasing and at the same time costs are rising. For many clergy there is also the problem that some parishioners think that any visit from the parish must be by the rector. The expectations on the clergy have not changed, even though lifestyle, culture, fewer clergy and increasingly ageing parishes make the calling much more difficult to fulfil. It is also important to note that some retired clergy can be unhelpful by their suggestion that all is needed is for the younger clergy to visit more and dress properly. I would ask them to remember that the society they ministered in has changed beyond recognition and simple answers are just not helpful. The legacy they left is one whereby people still expect clergy do to everything, and many of our people have never learnt the critical value of the ministry of all. In each and every generation, those who are called have sought to be faithful and, therefore, please pray for those today who have a very difficult, demanding and yet rewarding vocation.

My experience of parish ministry brought me the shadow of affirmation and support that were gifts of grace. These were gifts that I grieved for when I became a bishop. As a bishop I was no longer part of the support structure and bonds of affec-

tion of that community. I became the visiting preacher. In time
that has eased and the welcome I have received has been very
encouraging, but that has taken time. The shadow that brought
difficulty and struggle in parish life was the ever increasing
sense that radical steps were needed to ensure that we didn't
just maintain what we had, but enabled people to fly and grow
in order to extend the kingdom. The structure could function
well to maintain what we had, but that is not what our mission
is.

As I now reflect on parish life from a different perspective, as
the one who has the ministry of oversight, I find myself asking
very probing questions that do not have any obvious answers.
We need to hear the prophetic voice in the midst of our struggle,
to hear something of the wisdom of God as the Spirit guides us.
In the rest of this chapter, I want to share some of those questions
that revolve around the complexity of parish, ministry, mission,
diocese and the wider church.

I begin those thoughts with a quotation from a psychologist's advice to the parish system as he sees it: 'Stop clinging to
the positives. Let them float on the water. What can survive, will
survive. Face into the negatives. Develop the means to deal with
them; use the resources that exist. Trust the process of change.
Change is necessary and will occur whether it is welcomed or
not. To welcome change is to trust that the church always has
been, and will continue to be, a wise householder bringing out
treasures old and new.' (*The Future of the Parish System*, edited by
Steven Croft, p 31)

There is a recognition that many parishes throughout Ireland
are finding it more difficult to find the necessary finances and
numbers to maintain the ministry of the parish. These pressures
have led to parishes being joined in groups or unions so as to be
able to have an ordained ministry presence. It also leads to difficulties for clergy, bishops and parishioners as these groups or
unions can have difficulties that are not easy to resolve. It can
also lead to nervousness and fear when parishes become vacant.
Parishes are determined to do whatever it takes to keep their
parish and, in particular, to maintain their local church. As
someone who has ministered in a group of seven parishes when
I was a curate in Lecale, I understand the tensions and difficult-

ies of servicing seven centres of worship, keeping congregations content and ensuring the upkeep of so many buildings. Huge time and energy was needed to facilitate parish life and ministry and, unfortunately, mission was almost impossible. Bishop Michael Turnbull questions this practice: 'Bolting parishes together cannot go on without taking a look at the consequences. This policy has had a severe effect on the working patterns of clergy – probably to the detriment of pastoral care and evangelism – since clergy time is taken up with leading too many services, looking after several buildings and supervising duplicated electoral and administrative structures. We cannot continue on that road, as ministry in an alien situation will overwork and oppress the clergy, especially when they are working in isolation and running hard, at best, to stand still.' (In 'The parish system' published in *Ministry Issues for the Church of England*, by Gordon. W. Kuhrt, pp 213-4)

I believe that the parish is meant to be for those who don't belong. Increasingly parish life is dominated by those who belong, in seeking to maintain what we have; this is not a strategy for the future as it is only managing decline. The parish system as we have it needs to be more flexible and allow for difference, dependent on context and local needs. A full time ordained minister may not be the best model for ministry in every context, and therefore we need to change our diocesan regulations, and indeed the Constitution of the Church of Ireland, so that they can become tools to help us develop strategies for mission and growth. These are difficult issues and could easily become divisive but these questions must be asked and my real concern in raising them is that I do not have any obvious answers. There will have to be permission to experiment and even to fail. It strikes me that the patterns of church life in the New Testament were fluid, were being adapted in every situation, and were not without tensions and arguments. The problems that existed, the debates, the letters and the prayers, were genuine signs of life and growth. Perhaps I am showing my own preferences and personality type – I like grey and uncertainty, as from my perspective it allows for growth and can prevent restrictive rules and regulations.

One of the most obvious questions from a perspective of

oversight is the deployment of clergy throughout the church, and indeed of bishops. 'The church's management of its human resources – its most precious resource – is characterised by an incoherence in policy, aggravated by confused structures. In relation to the ordained ministry, for example, there is no single plan for the optimum numbers needed and how they are to be deployed, and for making the necessary plans for how the costs of their stipends and pensions are to be met. Ideally, the church should have a strategy which is mission-led rather than resource-led.' (*Strategic Church Leadership*, R. Gill and D. Burke, p 68)

The most precious resource the church has is its human resources, which are not just those who are ordained but also the ministry of the baptised. Do we always have to have an ordained person doing so many different roles within ministry, so often denying by default the ministry of all? From my experience in parish ministry, the role of a parish secretary, a youth worker and someone who had pastoral oversight of those in nursing homes and housebound in the parish, were wonderful gifts and an important statement of ministry not being dependent on the ordained. Alongside these roles, were the many, many volunteers who were the ministry of the parish and not just the ordained. It is one of the long term goals of the new Church of Ireland Institute to offer training for anyone involved in ministry of whatever form. From the perspective of oversight, equipping the saints must be a priority, and also to develop the structures to utilise their gifts for the mission of the church that is God-given.

For those in parish life, there are real tensions in trying to maintain buildings and ministry, with declining finances and resources. Within parishes there are the internal questions surrounding types of worship, the attempts to have children and youth ministries that are relevant and engaging without upsetting too many people; the desire to attract new families and yet a desire not to change too much. The role of those in leadership is fraught with struggle and frustration and I commend those who bear the heat and burden of the day. I believe they need to be supported and given permission to attempt new things and to dream dreams, but for too long their hands are tied by a structure that appears to be dedicated to stopping innovation and creativity. There is also the need for further training on managing change and how to engage with our culture and society to answer the questions they are asking, rather than the questions we wish they were asking. The task may appear daunting, but I believe this is a very exciting time to be in ministry and church life because the Spirit of God is stirring us, and circumstances, not least the financial crisis, is forcing us to reflect, think strategically and pray. It may be an uncertain future with a few metaphorical thunderstorms, but at the same time wonderful potential for mission and the building of the kingdom.

A difficult subject in our context, but critically important, is the need for ecumenical collaboration. One of the often unnoticed results of 'The Troubles' across Ireland is a much better co-operation and understanding of different traditions. This has happened by faithful people continuing to develop friendship and fellowship, despite the divisions in the wider community. The churches have faced criticism for being part of the conflict but I also believe they have been a very important bridge in enabling friendship and relationship across our divided society. In this context, some of the challenges in church life that lie ahead are to find more ways of collaborating, sharing resources that could include finances, buildings and people. This would enable a missiological strategy to extend the kingdom rather than defending denominations.

These are matters that have to be examined and questioned, as they are shadows that can stop others from seeing the glorious light of the one who is the light of the world. We are meant to reflect that light and incarnate his presence so that people can see and find him. Michael Riddell has some uncomfortable and yet important words for us: 'It is the form of the church in the West which has become the biggest barrier to the gospel. The broad sweep of our ecclesiastical life does not bear witness to the grace, passion, radicality, authority, tenderness, anger, excitement, involvement or acceptance of Jesus. Unfortunately the medium has become the message. The popular image of Christianity is formed by encounter with the church; and so Christianity is regarded as reactionary, oppressive, conservative, moralistic, hypocritical, boring, formal and judgemental.' (*Threshold of the Future*, p 39)

Perhaps the place we need to begin is by grieving for our shortcomings and praying for the grace to change. There is a temptation to defend ourselves and argue that we are facing a antagonistic culture and people are more cynical. I believe we are past the time of defending our diminishing influence and roles. We need to chart new waters and be willing to take risks with the various difficulties that will entail. However, the shadow of the presence of Jesus is with us, to give light and hope.

For those charged with oversight there is a very challenging future. Bishops need to be free to think strategically and not to just be managing the machinery and what is essentially decline. This is something I find demanding and difficult but it is critical for bishops and any church leaders at this stage of church history. 'It is the job of strategic leadership to bring the institution to make difficult decisions and make them in time. Realistic decisions can only be made when institutional priorities are clear and agreed – and that is why strategic planning is needed. Decisions also need to be made in time; not so late that the institution is exhausted, financially and in every other way. Otherwise there is no energy left for change.' (*Strategic Church Leadership*, R. Gill and D. Burke, p 28)

I can understand that sense of exhaustion. I have experienced it in parish life in seeking to maintain the parish system and in seeking to be innovative as well. As a bishop, I have also experienced that exhaustion, in seeking to keep the huge machinery of a diocese ticking over but also looking to the future and seeking to find a strategy for change and mission. These are demanding and difficult tasks and I have had to learn through time out that I cannot do it alone. There is the need for others to share the dream and to be committed to it.

The time to write these thoughts and reflections has also helped me rediscover that sense of call that started this journey for me, a reminder that this is God's church and God's mission and not mine or even ours. The God who has called us to be his church, despite our failings and inability to hear the still small voice, has promised to be with us and to guide us. There is no manual to follow, but an instruction to stay focused on the one who asks us to 'Follow me'. John Drane encourages and challenges me as I look to the future when he writes: 'If we truly

believe in a God whose primary attribute is creativity and imagination (Genesis 1:1-2:4a) – not to mention one who moves
mountains – then we can step out in faith into even risky spaces,
confident in the knowledge that we are not alone, and that God
may well already be ahead of us.' (*After McDonaldization*,
Preface, p xii)

CHAPTER NINE

A Taste of Heaven?

During my childhood I had a recurring dream, to put on the famous red shirt and walk out onto the hallowed turf of Old Trafford. For those who need this dream interpreted, I wanted to be a professional footballer and play for the team I have always supported, Manchester United. Obviously I didn't make it, like many thousands of others. However, I get to wear a scarf and go to watch them in that wonderful stadium. Indeed I have been known to watch them on television wearing my own shirt, a club shirt with my name printed on it and the number 7, in honour of Eric Cantona. This prized possession was a gift from the Knights of Columbanus after I spoke at one of their annual dinners. My thanks to them for their very personal gift that I cherish. There are many people who cannot understand this obsession and are bewildered and even appalled by it. Football and many sports are about personal preferences, family background and abilities. We make so many choices that are subjective and yet we are very passionate about them.

One of the shadows that has brought me joy and pain in almost equal measure is that of worship, what is meant to be a foretaste of heaven. Those beautiful, poetic and inspiring words from the Revelation to St John the Divine:

> You are worthy, our Lord and God,
> to receive glory and honour and power,
> for you created all things,
> and by your will they were created
> and have their being. (Revelation 4:11 *NIV*)

This is always a difficult subject for clergy, because everybody has an opinion and the views of people are subjective, and many do not have any patience with those who disagree with them or even worse, no desire to accommodate their ideas and aspirations. The discussions that rage around this subject can be very destructive to our common life and it is difficult to remember that, when we gather together for worship, we need to be aware of the visitor or stranger in the midst.

I have witnessed these heated arguments as a rector and as a bishop. As a rector I could seek ways to be creative and yet at the same time recognise the value of tradition. As a bishop it is more difficult because I have to recognise the tradition of every parish and I am not always aware of what happens in various local contexts. I also want to give clergy permission to experiment and be creative with the new liturgies, but that is not always easy to do and there may be limited resources. There are also many people in parish life who want to do what they have always done in their services of worship, and see me as the defender of tradition and certainly don't want me to encourage innovation. I find the question posed by Marva Dawn one that resonates with me:

> Can we find some way to prevent discussions about worship styles from becoming fierce battles waged between two entrenched camps? (*Reaching Out without Dumbing Down*, p 3)

There are many forms of these wars: from traditionalists to contemporary, catholic to evangelical, charismatic to formal, and organ to guitar, to name but a few. One of the often used arguments for change is that worship must be relevant in a rapidly changing culture. I think the argument ought to be that in everything, including our worship, we must be incarnational, not relevant. There is the danger that we mimic one of the prevalent cultural issues of everything being private and personal, by privatising faith and making it relative. This is highlighted by one of the trends of some modern faith songs that are about me and my feelings. The prayers of intercession can appear either as listening to one person talk to God or like a list of requests that are disjointed from everyday life. Even sermons can become more about the best joke rather than serious encounter with the text of scripture. There is a place for humour, indeed it would be great to see people in church allow their faces to show something of the joy that is meant to be ours, but we are not in the business of purely entertaining. Richard Bewes makes the following general observation about preaching today: 'Plenty of preaching in the West today is of an entertaining, joke-ridden nature; it is as if the church and the theatre have swapped roles. It is the theatre that tends now to take on the big themes that speak to the dilemmas of humanity, while the biggest-selling tapes at Christian conferences will often be from the speakers with the best jokes and banter.' (*Decision Magazine*, Sept/Oct 2005 issue)

Living with these tensions in parish life as a rector, and in a diocese as a bishop, has meant that often worship has become the source of an argument rather than something that can help and inspire me on my journey. Unfortunately, I believe, that this is true for many in ordained ministry. I have rarely been able to relax and enjoy worship because I have been responsible for it or leading it. There is also pressure on those who have responsibility for public worship to finish the service as quickly as possible. I believe the scripture should be read slowly and thoughtfully, prayers should be creatively led, (including music can be helpful). Worship should also allow for silence to enable us to hear the 'still small voice' of God. One of the most poignant moments in worship should be the collective saying of the Lord's prayer, when we recognise it is 'Our Father' and not just mine. Sometimes it is said so quickly it is hard to keep up.

These struggles with worship have been a shadow that has caused me difficulties in ministry and thereby on my journey of faith. However, there have been moments that have made me tingle with joy with the recognition of God's presence. In being a bishop I have been so privileged to ordain and confirm, and there is no greater sense of fulfilment. The delight of laying hands on people and praying for God's blessing is difficult to express adequately. The moments of quiet when I can attend an early morning service of Holy Communion in my local parish church, when I can be a member of the congregation, are special; the joy of the memorable moments when as a family we have prayed together; the quietness of the small space in our home where I can light a candle and be still to recollect God's presence. There were moments in parish life when together as a community of faith there was a collective sense of God's presence in our midst. These are moments that have inspired and helped me find light and peace.

Finding worship that isn't about issues or how we do it has become so important to me. Worship is about recognising God's presence and not about me finding God, because God is present, even when I don't recognise him. Bishop John Pritchard reflects on worship by writing: 'Worship is for God, to God and of God.' (*The Life and Work of a Priest*, p 12) People respond to worship according to personality, theological outlook and personal preferences. This is what can make it such a difficult subject and why sometimes people can get hold very strong views on the issue, because it is so personal to them. My friend and colleague Bishop Harold Miller writes: 'True worship is to do with both warm and personal faith and corporate, "common", communal expression. It is the desire of our soul. For some of us, we are warmed towards God most easily when we are in the company of other believers; for others we sense God's presence most strongly when quiet and alone . But for all Christians one feeds into the other, and we always pray "Our Father", even when in solitude.' (*The Desire of Our Soul*, p 13)

Worship has been both uncomfortable and comforting. There is that wonderful paradox in worship that God uses it to break us and to mould us. The restoration and forgiveness is experienced when there is brokenness and repentance. Worship is the space and time given to God for God to change us and heal us. It becomes the place where we are prepared to go forth to serve God in our neighbour. It will always include returning from the mountain top to the valley. There are times when we need the mountain top experience to cope with the pain and struggle of the valley.

The cycle of faith is present in worship. There should be the Good Friday and the Easter Day moments in worship. Bishop John Pritchard describes this in the following way: 'Worship is the moment when we we're both broken open and repaired at the same time. We're broken open to the majesty and love of God, to the beauty and angst of the world, and to the joyful detail of each other's lives. We're broken out of our self-enclosed, private worlds and place upon a bigger map and in a larger family. We can't truly encounter the living God and then go back to peeling the potatoes and cutting the lawn as if nothing had happened. At the same time, like a well-used piece of furniture, we're repaired by worship because the nails of our life and faith will often have worked loose during the week, and the glue will have come unstuck in places. What worship does is fit us together again, strengthening our joints and making us more 'serviceable' in God's work.' (*The Life and Work of a Priest*, pp 13-14)

The task for anyone responsible for public acts of worship is daunting and that is why it is disturbing when it becomes something that we can fight about so easily. This is a sad shadow for us as God's people. There must be a recognition of our own subjectivity and the need for variety, experimentation and creativity that enables us all, individually and collectively, to be restored and renewed for God's service.

One of the issues that is now recognised in the discussions about liturgy and worship is the building itself. Church buildings do play an important part in our worship. The building by its layout, lighting and furnishings can effect the various acts of worship held there. Most of our churches were built for large groups of people to join in public worship. Their layout often recognises a choir and clergy role in the worship that are separated from the congregation. The congregation are seated in such a way that encourages private devotion and little communal contact. They are places that don't recognise the presence of children as an important element of the community. The layout is also focused on a formal style of worship. Within my tradition we offer a cerebral liturgical style with structures that are full of words. These are not wrong but they do offer a particular style of worship and, certainly for young children and anyone with reading difficulties, they are not easy to follow.

In the diocese that I have the privilege of serving, we have the most wonderful buildings for worship but I believe we need to be creative in what we do with them. We have to find ways of making them more welcoming to the stranger, and creating spaces within the building that allows for different styles of worship. There are serious questions for the church of the twenty-first century to answer in how we use the public spaces we have. They are often in use for a few hours a week and are not as appropriate as they used to be, for our purposes in mission and ministry. An even more radical commentary is made by Barbara Brown Taylor: 'I worry about what happens when we build a house for God. I am speaking of the house of worship on the corner, where people of faith meet to say their prayers, because saying them reminds them of who they are, better than saying them alone. This is good, and all things cast shadows. Do we build a house so that we can choose when we go to see God? Do we build a house in lieu of having God at ours? What happens to the people who never show up in our houses of God?' (*An Altar in the World*, p 9)

Connected to the issue of buildings is the financial cost of the upkeep of buildings that are for a very limited use and how this can be such a drain on energy and money. Often parishes spend much of their income on maintaining a parish hall and a parish church and this is not necessarily good stewardship. I believe we need to be prepared to face some difficult issues to do with our buildings. They can be such a resource but only when they are fit for purpose. If we are to reconnect with the many who have disconnected from church, and sometimes from God, we have to find ways of using our buildings to give space and places for people to be welcomed and valued by those who are called to bring Christ's presence to all. This will involve imaginative planning and courageous decision-making by parishes and diocese. It will also involve changes in diocesan regulations and even the Constitution of the Church of Ireland. I believe there are very exciting opportunities, but I have found as rector and bishop our structures hamper us from being missional and keep us on a course of survival rather than change and growth.

The place of children in church is also a shadow that has concerned me as priest, bishop and especially as a parent. As a child my memories of church are hazy, but I was left with the distinct impression that what happened in church was for adults and children were tolerated and expected to be quiet and behave. The cynic might argue that for years they were seen and not heard and now they are neither seen nor heard. It is a worrying feature of parish life that it has become more unlikely to find children coming to church. Family services were thought to be a possible answer, but what about those without children and singles? Singing children's songs or getting them to read lessons or collect the offering is not engaging them with faith. I make this observation not just as someone who is ordained or as someone who enjoyed these acts of worship but particularly as a parent, because children were not expected to sit and be quiet. This was especially important for Liz, my wife, as she was essentially a single parent in church as I was at the front and of no use in helping her with our children in church. In fact, as she had grown up in a rectory and had experienced the expectations of being a clergy child in church, she found it even more difficult not to make our children resent church, never mind the more important matter of helping them love God. However, in my experience family services did not mean that our children's ministry flourished as a result. One of the most interesting results was that families worshipped once a month and did not see any need for their children to be any more involved in church activities. With the secularisation of schools and the school curriculum, these matters were and are an increasing shadow for the church and for me in ministry. In the baptismal liturgy the local church makes promises to all children that are baptised and I do worry that they are sometimes just words, as we often fail to find ways of ensuring that children are valued and given a special place in the life of the church which must include worship. The promise is as follows:

> We therefore receive and welcome you
> as a member with us of the body of Christ,
> as a child of one heavenly Father,
> and as an inheritor of the kingdom of God.
> (*The Book of Common Prayer*, p 366)

Every local faith community has a God-given responsibility to ensure the faith development of all who are baptised and that has massive and as yet unfulfilled implications for the place of children in the worshipping community.

I have always had a special affection for Elijah, not just because he struggled with God's call, but because he has left us with that wonderful moment recorded in scripture in 1 Kings 19:12, of the 'gentle whisper' or 'the still small voice'. Increasingly, I find the gift of silence critical on my journey. It is a shadow that offers me time and space to reflect and listen. Archbishop Rowan Williams writes: 'Silence somehow reaches to the root of our human problem, it seems ... Our words help to strengthen

the illusions with which we surround, protect and comfort ourselves; without silence, we shan't get any closer to knowing who
we are before God.' (*Silence and Honey Cakes: The Wisdom of the
Desert*, p 45) I find that silence re-energises and allows me time
to hear words of life rather than endless speech and noise. Those
moments of silence are important in the public acts of worship
as they give space and calm for the 'still small voice' to be heard.
'It is not so much that silence replaces words. Rather, through silence, words are allowed to recover their simple power and
truthfulness to bless and reveal.' (*Spirituality Workbook*, David
Runcorn, p 13)

One of the most important moments of silence in the liturgy
in the Church of Ireland is in the Eucharist where there is the
'Great Silence'. This is meant to be a time when we recognise the
wonder of God's amazing grace made known to us in the
'breaking of bread'. From my early years in church life, I was
never taught the wonder of this sacrament; my memory is of
people leaving in hoards at the end of Morning Prayer and a
handful people staying for communion. I remember as a teenager
being staggered by this as even then it struck me as the most important aspect of worship. Tragically the Eucharist has been a
shadow on my journey because it reminds me of the pain of division within the Body of Christ. But it has also become a shadow of grace and healing as I remember the wonder of God's
never-ending love and mercy. The Eucharist is a wonderful gift
of grace to all on the journey of faith with Jesus and it is a mystery that cannot be defined. Once we define the mystery we lose
the sense of wonder and awe that is the appropriate response to
Christ's command: 'Do this in remembrance of me.' 'Christ
makes himself known in the breaking of the bread. It is a place
where eyes are opened, where faith is renewed and divine life
and purpose are revealed.' (*Spiritually Workbook*, David Runcorn,
p 67)

It is my hope and prayer that together as communities of faith
we will be able to find ways of worshipping that help us find
ways of including children and the stranger. Ways of worship
that are not about our own preferences, but are about helping us
all find the amazing delight of experiencing God's presence.
That we will also rediscover the amazing gift that is ours in the

Eucharist, knowing the reality of Jesus' presence in our corporate and individual lives. 'First and foremost Christian worship is an epiphany of God. Christians meet in God's name. Jesus promised, "When two or three are gathered together in my name, I am in their midst." Worship is serious because it is a place where God manifests himself. But not the static, stone gods of Rome. This is the God of Abraham, Isaac and Jacob, and the Father of our Lord Jesus Christ. This is not a boring God, but the God of surprises.' (Quote from a sermon preached by Professor Bryan Spinks in Marquand Chapel on 14 April 1997)

CHAPTER TEN

The Shadow of Mystery

My memories of church when I was a child were that it was a place for adults and it was difficult as a child to engage with what was happening. It was a relief to be allowed to escape and go to Sunday School instead. During my teenage years as I was struggling to make sense of faith, the perception I had of God was of a remote and harsh figure who was disconnected from my life and from the world. Images of God were forming in my mind and being shaped by the people of faith and the context of church that I was experiencing. The religious culture of Northern Ireland, and the Protestantism that was an accident of birth for me, was making me question the kind of God being presented to me – the picture of an angry, judging God who was more concerned about saving me and others from hell than being concerned about me or the pain of the world. 'The particular image we have of God will depend very much on the nature of our upbringing and how we have reacted to it, because our ideas and our felt knowledge derive from our experience. If our experience has taught us to think of God as a policeman-like figure, whose predominant interest is in our faults, and if our encounters with him have been mostly in cold churches where we were bored out of our minds with barely audible services and sermons presenting God as he who disapproves of most things we like, then we are not likely to turn to him.' (*God of Surprises*, Gerard Hughes, p 36)

One of the shadows that has haunted me on my journey is that of guilt, of never being good enough. This is a result of my early experience of listening to the constant refrain of how my badness was what caused the death of Jesus. Slowly over the years the shadow has lifted in the light of God's amazing love. I am not loved because of anything I am or do, but because God is love. Jesus died not because of how bad I am but because of the

wonder and mystery of the love of the Godhead, expressed on
that first Good Friday. The shadow of God's grace is liberating
and frees me to be the unique person I am, made in the 'image of
God'. The negativity of so much preaching in the religious
world has been a shadow of control and manipulation, not allowing for questioning, searching or personal growth. My response to God is not out of fear or of the desire to avoid some
form of eternal punishment, but to experience the freedom of
what it is to be made in God's image. Therefore any response to
God is out of gratitude for that love and that is liberating, compared to a response of duty or fear. Too often religion seeks to
control rather than liberate, and it has been one of the struggles
on my journey to break free from images and perceptions of
God that were made by human imaginings. The wonder of the
God who loves is beyond our thoughts and images. Gerard
Hughes expresses this beautifully: 'We may construct a most
elaborate and ingenious religious system, but if it is not grounded
in this basic truth that God is mystery, then our elaborate system
becomes an elaborate form of idolatry. We are constantly tempted to make God in our own image and likeness. We want to control and domesticate him, giving him perhaps a position of great
honour in our hearts, home and country, but we remain in control. God is uncontrollable, beyond anything we can think or
imagine.' (*God of Surprises*, p 31) The question found in Isaiah
chapter 40:18, is left unanswered:

> To whom, then, will you compare God?
> What image will you compare him to?'

I believe in God but there are so many things that are beyond
my understanding. The God revealed to us in scripture is not
one we can define and describe adequately; this God is a God of
mystery, and the finite cannot understand the infinite. Words
from Isaiah describe this struggle:

> 'For my thoughts are not your thoughts,
> neither are your ways my ways,'
> declares the Lord.' (Isaiah 55:8)

The danger in defining God and ignoring mystery is that
there are so many questions we cannot answer. We then offer

pious platitudes to hide the confusion and do not allow for struggle and unanswered questions. Suffering is the greatest mystery for anyone, but for those with faith it poses particular difficulties. The randomness of human pain and tragedy leaves many in shock and despair. There have been some attempts to give answers to the awfulness of these moments, but I believe they often insult those in pain and paint an unhelpful picture of God. God can be portrayed as a God who picks on some people to test their faith. I have heard people comment that there is one more angel in heaven when a child dies. The religious culture that I grew up in appeared to deny the horror of the pain that some people experienced. To talk of heaven and afterlife as some panacea is not acknowledging the fact that we do not understand and that we do not have the answers to 'Why?' Job did not find any answers in his pain, but somewhere in the mess he found God's presence. I return to the incarnation: Jesus did not fix the suffering of the world but he pitched his tent in the middle of it and brought God's presence to it. I do not have any answers to those in pain, but I know that those who follow Jesus are meant to weep with those who weep and walk with them. Anne Lewin in her poem points to this mystery;

The Puzzle
The jigsaw pieces lie there, some
Jagged and broken by harsh treatment,
Others smooth from frequent handling.
Glowing with life and colour,
Some fall into place, others with
Little apparent meaning wait
Connections, or disentanglement
From wrong attachments.

Life's puzzle, with no master plan to guide,
Teases my understanding.
Some pieces pierce
With painful memory, some call out
Thankfulness and praise, others
I dare not contemplate, heavy with
Fear of what might be revealed.
Surrounded by mystery ,

I struggle to make sense of what I see.
If only I knew the mind of the designer.
(*Watching for the Kingfisher*, p 123)

It is impossible to describe adequately the God of scripture. We can reflect on the narratives and see patterns and discover incredible aspects of God's character. The ultimate understanding we have is in the word made flesh, Jesus as he lived among us affirming and redeeming our broken humanity. I have always enjoyed studying scripture and theology, but I always want to add a footnote that declares we can never fully understand. God is way beyond our understanding and thereby we are not called to a clear-cut intellectual clarity but to a relationship of love based on faith which leads us on a journey that never ends. 'The name, I AM THAT I AM, has been studied, examined probed, and meditated by an endless succession of scholars and saints in many languages in attempts to pin it down, define it, say what it means. God cannot be defined. 'Yahweh' is not a definition. God cannot be reduced to an 'object' of our inquiry or search. Is the name purposefully enigmatic? Revelational but not telling everything? Disclosing intimacy, personal presence, but preserving mystery, forbidding possession and control? I think so.' (*Christ Plays in Ten Thousand Places*, E. Peterson, p 159)

As I have journeyed with Jesus I have come to appreciate and value the symbols of faith and the rituals that have helped so many pilgrims through the centuries. These were not part of my religious inheritance – in fact I was taught to be suspicious of ritual and anything that might take the place of God. I was given a cerebral faith that did not experience ritual, sign or symbol. It was enough to believe and, above all, it was what I believe that mattered. Truth was measurable in a list of concepts and was one dimensional. This shadow was more complex because of the background of conflict in the community, a conflict that unfortunately had a religious context. The symbols and rituals of faith were often viewed as Roman Catholic, and Protestants didn't dabble with such things. Being Church of Ireland didn't necessarily help because, in the Northern Ireland setting, we were expected by most to be more Protestant. This shadow caused me to struggle. However, slowly but surely I came to value and appreciate some of those symbols and rituals that brought meaning and experience to my journey, removing some of the sterility of my religious background.

There are times when I am trying to pray for people and situations when I find it difficult to articulate my prayers and I find myself lost for words. Some years ago I found a prayer in Wells Cathedral when I was saying a prayer and lighting a candle.

> God, I light this candle
> because I am here;
> I don't know what to say,
> Don't know how to put my longings into words.
> You know who I light it for,
> those special people of my heart whom I love,
> and name before you.
>
> To light this candle, and leave it in this holy
> Place silently burning, comforts me.
> I see it as a small sign that love will always
> Live on, whatever happens.
> And that makes me
> Believe in you.
> Amen.
> (Patrick Woodhouse)

This prayer describes the beauty of lighting a candle and how it can help when words are difficult or even inadequate. In pastoral ministry, I have encouraged people who are struggling to articulate their prayers, to light a candle as a symbol of God's presence and light in their struggle and confusion. This use of symbol also reminds us of the mystery of faith, that there are questions we cannot answer and there are times we cannot make sense of what is happening, but we believe that the light of Christ shines in the darkness.

I also find it very helpful to keep a small wooden cross in the space in our home where I say my prayers, along with a few candles. Every evening when I come to the end of the day I find it liberating to write the names of people or situations that are troubling me on a post-it sticker and stick it to the cross. The symbolism is simple as I leave these people or issues with Jesus in the hope that I might get a good night's sleep. As I have journeyed with Jesus, one of the key lessons has been the reminder that only when I take time to recollect his presence can I find peace and strength.

Contemplative meditation has been something of a discovery for me on the journey, a shadow of light and help. This was not something I was introduced to until long after I was ordained. John Main describes meditation as follows: 'Meditation must be built into the everyday fabric of everyday life. It is being still, in a very simple child-like way, by paying attention.' (*The Expanding Vision*, edited by L. Freeman and S. Reynolds, p 17) There are many books written on the subject and yet the best piece of advice I have found is also by John Main: 'The less you talk about meditation the better. The real thing is to meditate.' (*Moment of Christ: The Path of Meditation*, John Main, p 97) Above all else, meditation is a reminder to me that I cannot do anything without God. It is the ultimate reminder that God is God. It is also a reminder of my humanity and brokenness.

This journey is not about our own efforts or self-control, it is primarily a gift, a gift of God to us in our struggling and questioning. A journey that has no end but it is marked by our successes and failures. It includes moments of wonder and delight as well as moments of fear and confusion. However, it is also about knowing that the most important shadow is Jesus and he is with us always. The words of Athenagoras describe the essence and hopes of this journey beautifully:

> I have waged this war against myself for many years.
> It was terrible,
> but now I am disarmed.
> I am no longer frightened of anything
> because love banishes fear.
> I am disarmed of the need to be right
> and to justify myself by disqualifying others.
> I am no longer on the defensive,
> holding onto my riches.
> I just want to welcome and to share.
> I don't hold onto my ideas and projects.

If someone shows me something better –
no, I shouldn't say better but good –
I accept them without regrets.
I no longer seek to compare.
What is good, true and real is always for me the best.
That is why I have no fear.
When we are disarmed and dispossessed of self,
when we open our hearts to the God-man
who makes all things new
then he takes away past hurts
and reveals a new time
where everything is possible.'

Athenagoras (Ecumenical Patriarch of Constantinople) as quoted in Jean Vanier, *Finding Peace*, p 59

CHAPTER ELEVEN

Shadows to Protect

Ordained ministry has been a constant process of learning and facing new situations and people. That brings an anticipation and excitement, but it also brings loneliness and some expect-ations that are unhelpful. I believe there is no greater privilege than this ministry. However, I also believe that it has become more difficult to exercise this ministry for many reasons. Some of the issues are cultural, disconnection from local communities, apathy, ageing congregations, the unwillingness to face change and the structures that make change more difficult. To exercise leadership and stewardship in any parish is demanding for all and for many exhausting.

From the perspective of having the oversight of a diocese, as a bishop, I have an increasing concern for the clergy and the lack of formal and structured support they are given. There is the need for a discussion on what might be done to support those who carry the burden of parish ministry. In this chapter I am going to examine some possible ways of offering shadows that can give time for reflection and support, amidst the constant de-mand of ordained life, which is a vocation and not a nine-to-five job.

Ordained ministry has some unusual tensions that differ from other working environments. Every parish provides their rector with a house, known as the rectory. These are usually large homes allowing for public space, especially a study. This is a mixed blessing as they are often older houses that are hard to heat and can be expensive for parishes to keep in good order. Yet they do provide the opportunity to live in the parish and be connected with the local community. However, it also means that keeping the boundaries between family and work is prob-lematical.

In my own experience, there was the complexity of being in a very public role in a local community while maintaining my own personal identity. There is the danger of performing a role that is expected, and in the process to hiding behind the position of rector and not being true to yourself. 'It is important to tell at least from time to time the secret of who we truly and fully are – even if we tell it only to ourselves – because we run the risk of losing track of who we are truly and fully, and little by little come to accept instead the highly edited version which we put forth in hope that the world will find it more acceptable than the real thing.' (*Telling Secrets*, F. Buechner, p 3)

With the constant demands of pastoral care, and especially being with those who are ill and bereaved, it is important to recognise our own internal struggles and needs. It is dangerous to be constantly giving to others without some form of self reflection and support. In other caring professions, there are structures to ensure the well being of those who care. To be able to examine what caring for others is doing to oneself in ministry is critical for self-protection. It is ironic for me to be writing these thoughts when I have had to take time off for what I can only describe as 'burn out', the emotional and spiritual exhaustion of thirty years of public ministry. When we are busy caring for others it can be easy to neglect, and even to fail to recognise, our own pain and turmoil. 'Even with the rabbuni so close – closer to us than we are to ourselves according to St Augustine – the power of self-deception and illusion can be overwhelming. Often the path disappears beneath us as we struggle with the demons of anger, fear, pride, greed and ignorance.' (*Jesus the Teacher Within*, L. Freeman, p 66)

Within the diocese of Connor there has been a pastoral support group for many years. This is a group of people with certain expertise and experience who are available to help clergy and their families on a confidential basis. The uptake of this support over the years has shown that there is an obvious need for clergy and their families to find help and counsel in the cauldron of parish life and ministry. This support has been particularly helpful in the crisis. However, they have also been looking at possible ways of developing more structured models of support, as well as still being available for any crisis. I believe it would be of great benefit to offer structured ongoing support to those who care for others, to help remove any sense of isolation and offer encouragement.

There is a support in ministry that I have used for years and it has been a shadow that has helped me when the busyness of doing has drained my spiritual resources. Spiritual direction has been defined in many ways but one of the most helpful phrases I have heard is the title of one of Kenneth Leech's books, *Soul Friend*. I have found the discipline important, in that it is a way of reflecting upon my journey of faith with Jesus that is at the core of my vocation and ministry. In the safe space that spiritual direction gives me, I give permission to another pilgrim, whom I respect, to probe my inner well being. The soul friend uses the gift of discernment to ask the appropriate questions as I reflect on my spiritual health. Henri Nouwen once defined the task of a spiritual director as: 'You're in a big room with a six-inch-wide balance beam in the centre. Now the balance beam is only twelve inches off the fully carpeted floor. Most of us act as if we were blindfolded and trying to walk on that balance beam; we're afraid we'll fall off. But we don't realise we are only twelve inches off the floor. The spiritual director is someone who can push you off that balance beam and say, "See? It's okay. God still loves you".' (quoted in *Soul Survivor*, Philip Yancey, p 287)

I believe it is critical not to underestimate the amount of emotional and spiritual energy needed for ministry. It is a role that demands so much from those who seek to be present for those whom they are called to serve. After seventeen years in one parish, I was very aware of the fact that each and every funeral and crisis call was becoming more difficult because of the fact that I had formed relationships and friendships with the people I was ministering among. I was part of a community where the bonds of affection were tangible and supportive, but in the pastoral crisis were costly to me. The space given for reflection with someone I respect and trust gives me recovery time and renews my energy. 'Spiritual direction refers to the structured ministry of soul care and spiritual formation in which a gifted and experienced Christian helps another person grow in relationship with and obedience to God.' (*Henri Nouwen and Soul Care*, W. Hernandez, p 19) I believe that everyone in ordained ministry should be offered this support, but for that to happen we need to train and equip more people to offer this valuable resource. It is not something that my own tradition has valued until recently.

There are other possible supports that I am only beginning to understand and use and I want to mention, recognising that my knowledge and experience is limited. They are supervision, mentoring and appraisal. I have always valued the friendship and prayers of those who are in ordained ministry and am grateful for that. However, I would also have to say that there are many times when I have been in the company of fellow clergy when we are not honest with each other about our struggles, and there can be an air of competition to see who appears to be the most successful. Clergy are human beings and are not free from jealousies and insecurities. I can assure you they are not super holy and free from the normal human reactions. 'Yet often when we get together we need help to deepen our conversation to a level beyond the superficial. If we are not telling success stories and trying to outdo each other with tales of how many hours we have worked without a break, then we are moaning about the structures and systems within which we work, or those who seem to have power over our lives. If the community of the church is to help us honestly reflect on our ministry, there needs to be some structure, some skill, some agreement or someone appointed to help us to be intentional in doing this.' (*Pastoral Supervision*, J. Leach and M. Paterson, p 9) There are key responsibilities in this role of supervision. They are about personal support, accountability in the professional role of public ministry, and ongoing professional and personal development. I would argue that this is about the duty of care the church has for those who are in the frontline of serving the church today in an increasingly secular and demanding culture. Within the diocese of Connor there has been a pilot project over the last two years, run with the experience and help of the Methodist Church through Edgehill College. This a programme of supervision for Church of Ireland rectors who have the privilege and responsibility of training curates and for Methodist Superintendents and probationers. It is to encourage those who supervise to develop appropriate structures and styles for supervision and to enable those beginning ordained life to see the importance of supervision in ministry. The following is a quote from the handbook devised for this by Edgehill College;

> Good definitions of supervision agree that:
> Supervision is a formal process.
> It is interpersonal, and can be undertaken one to one, in groups or peer groups.
> Reflection on the work of probationer/curate is central to supervision.
> Its goals include greater professional competence.

The initial response has been positive and I certainly hope that this can be offered to all clergy so as they can continue to reflect upon their practice and the need for life-long learning and training, in a rapidly changing context for mission and ministry. As I return to ministry after my recovery, I have pledged to have someone to supervise me, to enable me to have that professional care for me and the calling that I now seek to fulfil. Supervision has been adopted and found of great benefit in other denominations and indeed in other parts of the worldwide church. The Uniting Church in Australia published a document in 2001 and the following excerpt is illuminating: 'The desired outcome of truly pastoral supervision is a continuing enhancement of the ministry offered. Along with this can go increased self-respect, released potential, the capacity to see, feel and hear what has not been seen, felt or heard, and the bonuses of increased health and well-being and increased effectiveness in ministry. Research shows a high correlation between good supervision and vocational satisfaction.'

Reflecting on the last three and a half years as bishop, I am very conscious that I arrived in post with very little idea of what I was expected to do as bishop. In fact when I became a young rector at twenty-nine years of age, I was very aware of suddenly being on my own, without the support of a rector and the comfort of somebody else being ultimately responsible for the parish. I remember the night of my institution in Helen's Bay when the bishop, the clergy, our friends and our wider family circle went home and there was the realisation that Liz and I were on our own to start all over again at establishing friendships and trying to remember everyone's name. Now as bishop when I leave an institution service of a new rector I am very conscious that I am leaving someone to the loneliness of leadership and parish ministry. I believe there is a model that could be useful for new rectors and definitely for new bishops. 'Mentoring is a process not dissimilar to apprenticeship, by which we take a (usually) younger or less experienced person, (usually) in our own field of work or life, and travel alongside them (usually) for a medium to long period of time with the purpose of helping them to maximise their potential.' (From an Arrow Ireland booklet entitled *Mentoring Resources*, p 1) It is the concept of someone who understands the role but, even better in my mind, is someone who has experience in doing it. I would like to move towards the place as a diocesan bishop that every new rector has a mentor to walk with them in their early years of their new position. Diane Clutterbuck describes the place of a mentor in a very insightful way: 'A mentor is a more experienced individual, willing to share his/her knowledge with someone less experienced, in a relationship of mutual trust. A mixture of parent and peer, the mentor's primary function is to be a transitional figure in an individual's development.' (*The Mentoring Kit*, Henley Distance Learning.) One of the creative side-effects of mentoring would be to develop a bond between experienced and inexperienced clergy and could therefore build up the collegiality in a diocesan team of clergy.

Some years ago when I was a rector in the diocese of Down and Dromore, Bishop Harold Miller encouraged a pilot project of clergy self-appraisal, which was described as a ministry review. This was an attempt to encourage an opportunity for personal growth and self-awareness, to assist clergy in an objective assessment of their lives and ministry. In the document that was given to clergy to take part in this project, the following introductory comments were recorded:

Affirm the good – skills, gifts, positive developments and satisfying aspects of ministry.
Reflect on all aspects of experience so as to learn from them.
Resolve to take appropriate action so that there is continued growth, change and development.
Review your ministry.

This pilot scheme was carried out by people with experience in staff development who were not ordained, and most found it very helpful and affirming. However, it has to be acknowledged that it was difficult to facilitate because of the need for experienced and competent people to implement it on a much wider scale.

These are possible ways of offering structured support to clergy as they seek to fulfil their vocation, and should be recognised as necessary ways of helping those who give so much and yet are very often not recognised by the institution as having been faithful.

There are other shadows that need to be examined for the future development of church life, giving ways of ensuring time and energy is not wasted fighting internal battles in parish life that are so debilitating for everyone. Other churches have been examining a code of conduct for clergy, and there also needs to be a code of conduct for all members of the church. These are becoming more important because of the different and more vulnerable place clergy can now find themselves in. There would also be protection for non-ordained members of the church from being taken for granted or being maltreated in any shape or form.

The various models of support mentioned in this chapter are meant to be shadows to protect all involved in church life, as so many can feel alone and unsupported in the cut and thrust of parish life and ministry, and not just those who are ordained. We need to relax in God's call and constantly reflect upon it rather than always being frenetically busy and asking others to do the same. 'In our zeal to proclaim the Saviour and enact his commands, we lose touch with our own basic and daily need for the Saviour. At first it is nearly invisible, this split between our need of the Saviour and our work for the Saviour. We feel so good, so grateful, so saved. And these people around us are in such need. We throw ourselves recklessly into the fray. Along the way most of us end up so identifying our work with Christ's work that Christ himself recedes into the shadows and our work is spotlighted centre stage. The work may be wonderful, but we ourselves turn out to be not so wonderful, becoming cranky, exhausted, pushy and patronising in the process.' (*Under the Unpredictable Plant*, Eugene Peterson, p 114)

CHAPTER TWELVE

The Constant Shadow

This journey has been an adventure that has meant I have met some wonderful people and been in some beautiful places, but it has also caused me turmoil and confusion and at times made me struggle, particularly with people who profess to be Christian. There has been one constant shadow on the journey and that has been the presence and grace of Jesus. That grace has become all the more important as I have sought to exercise leadership in the church. There has never been a time when I didn't believe, but there have been times when I have wrestled with faith and with the vocation I have sought to follow. One of the key lessons that I have had to learn is that faith is not about *what* I believe but *in whom* I believe. Faith for me is not about a list of concepts or statements of faith, but about a relationship with Jesus who has helped me understand something of the wonderful mystery that is God. Albert Schweitzer describes this relationship: 'He comes to us as One unknown, without a name, as of old, by the lake-side, he came to those men who knew him not. He speaks to us in the same words: "Follow me!" and sets us to the tasks which he has to fulfil for our time. He commands. And to those who obey him, whether they be wise or simple, he will reveal himself in the toils, the conflicts, the sufferings which they shall pass through in his fellowship, and, as an ineffable mystery, they shall learn in their own experience who he is.' (*The Quest of the Historical Jes*us, p 403)

In this chapter I want to reflect upon some of those insights that I have found helpful on my journey with Jesus as I have sought to journey with him. The Christmas story as recorded in the gospels has wonderful material for a fairy story, and sometimes when we celebrate Christmas we appear to have turned it into just that. The portrayal of the beautiful crib scene with a clean stable and parents who look positively angelic can make a

nonsense of the miracle. Anne Lewin's poem; 'Nativity Scene',
points beyond idealised Christmas cards:

'Crib Figures take care',
The notice said.

The power of your simplicity,
Grouped there in silent
Adoration, could leave us
Most dissatisfied. Take care –
We cannot bear too much
Uneasiness. But keep us
Mindful of the hope
Embodied in that child,
Lest we allow it to shatter
Like a Christmas toy. Above all,
Keep us from underestimating God,
(*Watching for the Kingfisher*, p 43)

The mystery of Bethlehem fills me with wonder and joy. This
is a God I can relate to, who comes to us and dwells among us.
God did not come to fix all the mess of human existence, but
came to share our humanity that we might in turn share something of God's divinity. God in Jesus came and pitched his tent
among us and thereby affirms our broken humanity. This is not
a harsh, judgemental God like some kind of remote and uncom-
promising judge, but a God of amazing compassion and care for
creation in its totality. To come in the form of a tiny helpless
baby, who cried, despite the words of the Christmas carol that
says 'no crying he makes'. This is a God who isn't detached
from human pain but understands it and experienced it.
Bethlehem is the incredible expression of love, and yet the mystery of this moment baffles us as God becomes vulnerable and
fragile. This is a God who turns things upside down, who con-
fuses the wise and welcomes those who become like little children, accepting the wonder and beauty of simplicity. The difficulty is that so often those of us who believe try to define the
mystery, and lose the wonder. 'The doctrines of the incarnation
and deity of Christ are meant to tell us that we cannot start with
a predetermined, set-in-stone idea of God derived from the

Bible, and then extend that to Jesus. Jesus is not merely intended to fit into those predetermined categories; he is intended to explode them, transform them, alter them for ever and bring us to a new evolutionary understanding of God. An old definition of God does not define Jesus: the experience of God in Jesus requires a brand-new definition of God.' (*A New Kind of Christianity*, Brian McLaren, p 150) The Jesus that I was introduced to as a child was two-dimensional and wooden; the Jesus I have come to experience is someone I can never fully know or understand, is full of surprises and is quick to challenge my preconceived ideas of God and of other people. The Jesus that I have discovered journeying with me is someone who believes in me, is a risk taker and is much more radical than I had imagined. 'I suggest we think historically about a young Jew, possessed of a desperately risky, indeed apparently crazy vocation, riding into Jerusalem in tears, denouncing the Temple, and dying on a Roman cross – and that we somehow allow our meaning for the word 'god' to be recentred at that point. (*The Challenge of Jesus*, N.T. Wright, page 92.)

In the four gospels there is a collection of encounters, miracles, teaching and withdrawals. Each one of the gospels gives us different angles on the impact Jesus had on those closest to him and on first century first Palestine. Jesus declares a vision of God's kingdom that was already present. However, his communication and teaching style leaves us with homework to do, and also the prayer that the Holy Spirit will teach us, as we seek to discover what his words mean for us today. The parables and the images he uses leave us to listen and to hear, to work it out for ourselves, unlike some preaching I have been subjected to. Bishop John Pritchard highlights Jesus teaching style: 'What Jesus presented was not a coherent platform for a religious campaign. He offered a set of metaphors, images and stories to challenge his listeners at the deepest level of the imagination, where visions grow, dreams are cooked slowly, and courage matures into action.' (*Living Jesus*, p 29)

In reading the gospels and trying to understand the depth of what Jesus is saying, it is critical to understand the context. To know something of the context of a younger son asking the father for his inheritance, brings alive the horror of the implications of what the son was asking for: 'I wish you were dead.' Which highlights the wonder of the father running to greet the son when he was along way off. To grasp the importance of the elder brother in the context of Jesus' conflict with the religious leaders of his day is vital. They were standing outside complaining about his grace to sinners and outcasts.

The parable of the Good Samaritan is not simply about being a good neighbour, but it is to recognise the uncomfortable truth that we have to especially recognise those we don't value or accept as our neighbour. These hidden depths lead us to such rich treasures that show Jesus as being much much more than a good teacher of morality, but someone who profoundly challenges what it is to be human and to be made in the image of God. 'Jesus keeps our feet on the ground, attentive to children, in conversation with ordinary people, sharing meals with friends and strangers, listening to the wind, observing the wildflowers, touching the sick and wounded, praying simply and unselfconsciously. Jesus insists we deal with God right here and now, in the place we find ourselves and with the people we are with. Jesus is God here and now.' (*Christ Plays in Ten Thousand Places*, E. Peterson, pp 33-4)

The encounters Jesus has with various people, as recorded by the gospel writers, are fascinating. There is such a warmth, honesty and acceptance. The rich young ruler is told the truth and yet affirmed at the same time. The woman caught in adultery is challenged but supported. She discovers the wonder of amazing grace that stood by her and with her and gave her another chance, and yet never condoned what she did. I have found the shadow of this Jesus to be affirming and gracious with my brokenness, and always offering me forgiveness and mercy. Jesus did not pressurise people to believe or to conform to particular dress codes or behaviour before he loved them. This love as I read about it, and as I have experienced it, is unconditional and that is not something humanity is used to. Too often in our retelling the message we have introduced conditional love, whereby people have to do certain things before they will know this love. It is always there and available and has been declared for all eternity, not just on a piece of wood in the form of a cross but in the word made flesh. In his encounters with people Jesus lived out this unconditional love and it transformed people. It did not control them through fear or guilt but liberated them through affirmation and hope. 'He simply let the people know he liked them – and so did God, that he was interested in them, that they didn't have to be ashamed of who they were. He came close to them in their illnesses, wept with them at the graves of their loved ones, ate at their tables, drank their wine, listened to their words, let himself be injured by their pain – and, although it isn't recorded in any of the gospels (canonical or otherwise), I imagine he laughed at some of their jokes too. (*Everything Must Change*, Brian McLaren, p 280)

I have also found Jesus to be a patient teacher, allowing me to make mistakes and often the same ones, yet forgiving and encouraging me to try again. The relational leadership style of Jesus is clearly seen with the disciples. He wanted them to learn for themselves and not just accept what he taught them. He was alongside the disciples, modelling a servant leadership. Yet he also taught them the importance of boundaries, when he would go off to a quiet place to pray, to recharge and to prepare for the next part of the journey. The rhythm of his ministry is that of being in the busyness of the market place with people, and also of withdrawing to the desert for stillness and recovery. Too often I have lost sight of just being with Jesus, and allowed the busyness of doing to dominate. Busyness is one of the greatest dangers of ministry and discipleship: it can exhaust us and prevent us from recognising that all important truth of John 15:5b: 'Apart from me you can do nothing.' From my own religious culture and background, I was encouraged to be busy for Jesus, but I have to learn that what really matters is to stay close to Jesus, to stop trying to prove myself and carry impossible burdens but to rest in him. The resting in him can enable us to be the person we are meant to be and not some frazzled disciple, exhausted and burdened.

'Jesus, gentle and humble in spirit, invites us. It is not a free lunch. There is a yoke … but it is easy:
It is not the yoke of Pharaoh's bricks or Jewish law or Roman demands or capitalist exploitation or Presbyterian rigor;
It is an easy yoke of trusting discipleship. Sabbath from the hard yoke is to take the easy yoke of becoming who we are meant to be.'
(Walter Bruggemann, *Mandate to Difference*, p 46)

In my journey I have found myself more and more drawn to silence as I seek to follow him. Words have become less important as I meditate and listen to the still small voice. There is that wonderful moment when Jesus stands before Pilate and his silence is deafening. Just before the beginning of his public ministry Jesus is in the wilderness for forty days listening to the silence. Silence is uncomfortable but when used as part of praying it is creative and life-giving. Silence isn't just an absence of noise but it is a recognition that God is within us and, as we are still and quiet, we might just hear those words of affirmation and acceptance. These are not audible words, at least they never have been for me, but there is a profound sense of calm and wellbeing as we rest in the presence of the one who loves us. There is the wonderful image of the psalmist that describes this stillness:

> I have stilled and quietened my soul;
> Like a weaned child with its mother. (Psalm 131:2)

The discipline of contemplative mediation has also been a shadow of light for me. I have never found it easy, but as someone who gets their energy from within rather than from others, this quiet listening has been restorative. The quiet and gentle repetition of scripture allows the word to take root deep within. John Main has been an inspiration to many on this road and his words are enlightening: 'It is so easy to live our lives in some mechanical way, going through routines each day, but losing the sense of freshness, of creativity and freedom. As a result, we live our lives in a sort of a rush, one routine following the next, distracted perhaps for a bit by entertainment, by pleasure, or deadened by the pressure of work or play. To break out of this cycle, each one of us must learn to stop the rush of activity. We must learn the priority of being. We must learn to be still. That's what our regular times of meditation are about.' (*John Main: The Expanding Vision*, edited by L. Freeman and S. Reynolds, p 23)

At the heart of the good news we declare and seek to live by, is the ultimate paradox that out of the awfulness, the literal hell of Good Friday, comes the miracle and wonder of Easter Day. Death and resurrection are intrinsically linked, sorrow and joy, struggle and peace. The shadows I have experienced on the journey with Jesus have contained paradox. They have been both light and darkness and I believe we cannot have one without the other. As in Bethlehem so on the outskirts of Jerusalem, God acts in ways that are not what anyone expected. The torment of the cross I have never understood, but I do not believe that God was so angry with human sinfulness that he punished Jesus. It was love that died and rose again, not anger. It was forgiveness not vengeance. I cannot understand the mystery of God's redeeming love: 'If humanity killed the one who fully embodied God's intention for our lives, and God still loves us, then there is no need to earn God's love.' (*The Powers That Be*, Walter Wink, p 92)

The early stage of my journey with Jesus was lived out with the backcloth of the viciousness of sectarian bombing and killings with a religious dimension. I witnessed religion that appeared to hate rather than love, that wanted revenge rather than mercy and that wanted exclusion rather than embrace. Yet this flies in the face of the amazing declaration by God in the good news of that first Easter, amidst the paradox of death and resurrection. The Jesus I have sought to journey with had and still has a radical message that wasn't just words, but was lived out by his life and particularly in his death. Jürgen Moltmann describes this radical new worldview when he writes: 'The one (Jesus) will triumph who first died for the victims and also for the executioners, and in so doing revealed a new righteousness which breaks through the vicious circles of hate and vengeance and which, from the victims and executioners, creates … a new humanity.' (*The Crucified God*, p 178)

It is fascinating when I look back on the early years on this journey: I had answers to so many questions, or at least I thought I did. I have far fewer answers now, but I am more than ever convinced of Jesus, the one who has brought me peace in the confusion, joy in the sorrow and a growing confidence in the wonder of being a child of God, accepted and loved for who I am.

A few years before I became a bishop I had the joy of welcoming Bishop Jimmy Moore and his wife Mary to Ballyholme after he retired. He had been my archdeacon many years before he became Bishop Of Connor. He was such an encourager and friend, a man of wisdom and prayer. Unfortunately he died after a few years of retirement and not long before I became a bishop. I was honoured and thrilled that his family gave me his Episcopal ring, which I am delighted to wear. I have had it inscribed with the question Jesus asked of Peter recorded in John 21:17: 'Do you love me?' That is the ultimate question for those who are seeking to follow Jesus. This journey is a relationship of love and it is critical, no matter who we are or what our calling, that we remain in love with Jesus, because it is out of that love that we are called and it is in that love that we can fulfil his calling.

> Nothing is more practical than finding God, than falling in love in a quite absolute way, final way. What you are in love with, what seizes your imagination, will affect everything. It will decide what will get you out of bed in the morning, what you will do with your evening, how you spend your weekends, what you read, whom you know, what breaks your heart, and what amazes you with joy and gratitude. Fall in love, stay in love, and it will decide everything. (Fr Pedro Arrupe SJ, General of the Society of Jesus.)

CHAPTER THIRTEEN

The End and the Beginning

The wise men came to Bethlehem
by following a thread of light
that led them to a sleeping child.
And though we tried to drown that quiet
by hammering the child to twisted wood,
and pushing thorns into his scalp,
yet in the quietness of the dawn,
without a sound,
without a single movement of the air,
he slipped out of death,
left his grave-clothes on the side,
and went to play his whooping games
with astonished and familiar angels.

Yet though heaven may resound to his eternal play,
God still treads softly here,
Listen!

(from the poem 'God Treads Softly Here', published in *God Treads Softly Here*, by Trevor Dennis, p 66)

There are various signs of the ageing process – the extra pounds or kilos, the receding hairline and longer arms. I noticed I needed longer arms when I was trying to read anything from a book to a menu. The moment came when I was in church and I stood up to read the gospel – I couldn't see it no matter how much I stretched my arms. Mercifully it was a well known passage and I was able to wing it. I now wear reading glasses and I am so dependent on them that I keep an old pair in the car in case I arrive somewhere without my specs.

Writing these thoughts has helped me see things more clearly. It has crystallised my thoughts. I have found a renewed sense of vocation to be a disciple and to be ordained. This has come about because of the space I have been given to recover from the exhaustion of doing. I am very grateful to those friends who have walked with me, not least my family, Liz, Peter and Ruth, they are such special gifts to me.

I have always found the Psalms a treasure trove of human emotions and spiritual exclamation, and even question marks. One of their delights is that they express the depths of spiritual probing and struggle. Psalms 42 and 43 end with the words:

Why are you so downcast, O my soul?
Why so disturbed within me?
Put your hope in God,
for I will yet praise him,
my Saviour and my God.'

There can be many reasons why we can struggle on the journey. The shadows that can hide the light are different for each traveller, but the depth of the emotions are similar. Some of the teaching I heard when I was younger would have encouraged me to stay strong and one day all would be well. This appears to me to have been a form of anaesthetic, or of a life-jacket to get me to the afterlife. However, I have found it more helpful to wrestle with faith, to question, to probe and even at times to express my frustration and anger with God. Why is there so much pain in the world? Why do children have to die? Why do people have to starve? Unfortunately I haven't any answers, but I have found the ever present shadow of Jesus with me and I believe he is longing for the restoration of the whole of creation. He also has called the church, with all its brokenness and fractures, to witness to his grace and love. We have much to do and especially to help restructure our local church life to make it fit for purpose.

Easter is the constant reminder of new beginnings and of life out of death. One of the first steps for many of us is to admit we are struggling, and thereby find the grace of new beginnings. When we face the inner turmoil of past failures and unfulfilled dreams, they are a difficult and important reminder to us of the need to stay close to Jesus. Richard Rohr describes this lesson in a different way: 'We do not really know God except through our own broken and rejoicing humanity.' (*Everything Belongs*, p 19)

The disciples, as they walked to Emmaus on that first Easter Day, understood the words of Psalm 42 and 43. From their religious inheritance these words would have been known to them. They were desolate, bewildered and angry. The events that they had just witnessed did not make sense. They were also in grief, they had witnessed the one they loved die. The shock was setting in, they were finding it difficult to verbalise their loss and to make sense of the events. There was a stranger who journeyed with them and they didn't recognise him. He shadowed them on their way and listened to their angst and hurt. Gently and wisely he opened their minds to see the events from a different perspective. The story was no longer to be understood from their perspective of the events. They were now seeing the events from the upside down and inside out perspective of a crucified and risen Jesus. Yet there was a further twist to the events that day, before they opened their eyes to see the past few days through different lenses. 'Following Jesus' astonishing exposition of scripture, they come into the house; Jesus takes the bread, blesses it and breaks it, and their eyes were opened, and they recognised him.' (*The Challenge of Jesus*, N. T. Wright, p 125) There, in that simple and mysterious eucharistic moment, they recognised the stranger as the 'Risen Jesus'.

There are particular elements to the Emmaus record that I find illuminating: friendship, scripture and Eucharist. The disciples had each other as they journeyed, they had the gift of friendship that enabled them to share the pain and disappointment with each other and the stranger. The gift of fellow travellers is a very special gift as we journey with Jesus. We are not meant to journey on our own. One of the dark shadows from my early years of faith was the overemphasis on God as being all I needed. God will not be concerned when I say as a human being I need the encouragement of my brothers and sisters as I travel and learn to trust and strengthen faith. One of the dangers of our cultural inheritance, from a faith perspective, is that we are very proficient when it comes to talking about the weather. However, talking about our journey with Jesus is too embarrassing or only for the very religious and intense. The gifts of encouragement and affirmation are neglected gifts within the body of Christ, as we are meant to build one another up in love. 'Whether taking up new responsibilities of leadership or continuing in service, we all need mentors and friends to guide and inspire, to challenge and support us as we live and work. Leadership is risky business. It takes more from the servant leader than it gives. We need one another.' (*Relational Leadership*, Walter Wright, p 27)

There have been many suggestions about what particular scriptures Jesus, the stranger, might have used with the disciples on this journey. This use of the scriptures enabled the disciples to see the preceding events from a new perspective. The important issue for me is that the scriptures became lenses for new insights. There was a recognition that new lessons could be learned and new understanding gained. Scripture is a wonderful gift, but it can also be a dangerous weapon. Within our religious culture it can be used to exclude and hurt, without careful explanation. However, it is a special tool for the journey as it reveals to us the living word, Jesus, who is the word made flesh. I was helped to discover the study of the scripture early on my journey of faith, by people who taught me the importance of the Bible. The scripture is not to be worshipped in itself, but it is to point us to the one who is to be worshipped and glorified forever.

That moment of recognition was transformative. They recognised him as he broke the bread. It is only over time on the journey that I have come to treasure the Eucharist. Part of the religious legacy that I was given in my youth meant that I didn't recognise then how important the sacrament was. It was always something that divided people within the Christian community and arguments over the mystery of Eucharist were and are sad. It is difficult to define something that is of God, that is a channel of God's grace. I find it such a source of grace and strength when I receive the body and blood of Christ. It is a constant reminder of the journey Jesus had when he came and dwelt among us. It is also a reminder that he still journeys with me and his people today and everyday. 'We hold out open hands and receive what God does for us in Jesus. In receiving the Eucharist we relive, remember, the Exodus Passover and the Last Supper. Each time we receive the Eucharist we again let Jesus take us with him into the comprehensive drama of his death and that pulls us as praying participants into the life of salvation. Before we do anything for God, we receive what God in Christ does for us.' (*Christ Plays in Ten Thousand Places,* Eugene Peterson, p 200)

The disciples as they journeyed were transformed. They had to leave behind the shadows that left them broken and hurting. Through friendship, the scriptures and the breaking of bread they discovered the constant shadow who was with them all along.

Our story is rooted in their story and that is a story we need to retell to each and every generation. It is God's story, the scriptures reveal to us a lovesick God seeking to love all of creation into life and light. What a story! Resurrection wasn't the end, only another beginning or the continuation from a different perspective.

> On the road to Emmaus,
> in a small house,
> in a room,
> at a meal,
> that ancient intimacy was found again.
> We call that rediscovery
> 'resurrection'.
> (From 'The Walk to Emmaus', in *The Three Faces of Christ,* Trevor Dennis, p 55)

So I return to the beginning and it is also the end. We return to Emmaus and the life-changing discovery of those who were on a journey on the first Easter morning. Their shadow of death and despair became the shadow of life and hope. May we all know the shadow of Jesus with us as we experience his light to the shadows that bring us darkness.